FEARLESSWOMEN

MIDLIFE PORTRAITS

NANCY ALSPAUGH AND MARILYN KENTZ

PHOTOGRAPHY BY

MARY ANN HALPIN

STEWART, TABORI & CHANG | NEW YORK

CONTENTS

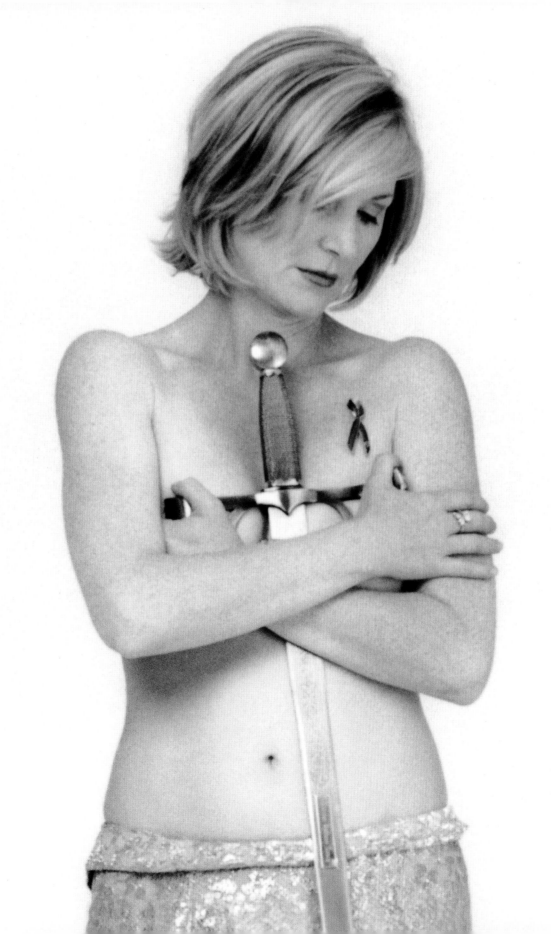

INTRODUCTION

WHEN THE THREE OF US—Mary Ann, Marilyn, and Nancy—set out to create an inspiring book about and for women in the middle of their lives, one boldly and aptly named *Fearless Women*, we had no idea what it would bring. By exploring the lives of "fearless women," we hoped first of all to draw attention to the fact that so much has changed for women in the twenty-first century. Fifty years ago, sixty was considered old age, and a woman turning forty was thought to be on a downward slide. But with today's medical advances and healthy lifestyles, women are living longer and making the most of the productive, fulfilling years before them. For many women now, turning forty offers new opportunities, a chance to reflect on younger years and explore the possibilities ahead. We wanted to honor those who are redefining midlife. So we began our journey to find women ages forty- to sixty-something who discovered, in their middle years, newfound opportunities to make a real difference.

It took us a year to gather fifty representatives who demonstrate that midlife is our prime time. We found great women who understand that time and experience are the prerequisites for becoming the strong beings they are now, inspiring other women their age to stand tall and proud—fearless, even. The women we met and photographed have not shied from the light or considered themselves washed up, but instead revel in their heightened passion, have an unquenchable thirst for life, savor their wisdom, trust in their incredible insight, and simply overlook their baggy knees.

We found them in all walks of life. Some who might have seemed ordinary on the outside proved to have extraordinary attitudes.

Some who pushed through personal hardship then used their experience to make a difference in others' lives. They came from rural areas, small towns, cities, and suburbs. Some could have been the woman next door. Some were of the Hollywood elite. All prove that women, no matter what their age, are the nurturers, creators, and caretakers of the world—and all feel they are at their best now.

For this book, we asked each participant to express her power by holding a sword—a symbol of courage. We also asked each woman to share a snapshot of herself in her twenties, at the time in life when society suggests that women are most desirable. But as women who have been there ourselves, we know that what lies under that silky, glowing skin is often something other than perfection. In our twenties, some of us looked exquisite on the outside but had a lot of growing up to do on the inside. Some of us were insecure approval-seekers, some were struggling to come to terms with a desperate childhood, and some were basking in a little too much vanity. Comparing ourselves with who we were in our youth and discovering that our lives are much better today blows apart the myth that it's all downhill after forty.

Convincing society of this, however, proved to be a bit tricky, especially when celebrities were involved. When we began contacting the representatives of the famous women we wanted to honor, we found that once the word *midlife* came into play, the celebrities were often suddenly out of town. Is it any wonder, when these women have to compete in an entertainment business that casts men in romantic leading roles opposite actresses young enough to be their granddaughters?

But we did find some well-known personalities who love what we're doing. These awesome women defied conventional Hollywood thinking to participate in this book, holding their swords tight and heads high. That alone made them fearless, but that's not why we chose them. We wanted to honor those who use their influence to make a difference. We found television stars who became goodwill ambassadors, icons who created foundations to save wildlife, and famous names who spend most of their time raising money to support families of Alzheimer's victims.

Fittingly, each of us happened to be going through our own midlife challenges during the making of this book: Mary Ann had to have emergency surgery as well as tend to the needs of her eighty-one-year-old mother, who was healing from a serious car accident. Marilyn was dealing with empty-nest heartbreak as her youngest daughter prepared for college. And Nancy was performing a balancing act as an exhausted forty-nine-year-old working mother of an energetic two-year-old. But during the course of the photo sessions, something magical happened. Certain moments put everything in perspective. When we saw the actress Shohreh Aghdashloo posing in a dress made in her native Iran, where the mere mention of her name is banned, and heard about how she fled the country seeking freedom, we were awestruck by her depth and beauty and her graceful dance with the sword. After the photo session, Shohreh took her good-luck necklace off and tearfully gave it to Mary Ann. When Catherine Curry Williams sat on a bench next to a teddy bear that symbolized her deceased newborn son, we were moved to tears. When Kathy Eldon, another member of the sisterhood of grieving mothers, posed holding a dove named Peace with a shaft of light over her right shoulder, she said it looked as if her son, Dan, was looking down from heaven. Somehow we knew that these passages were simply a part of the cycles of our lives, and we felt so lucky to experience them. These moments taught us to dance with the dark figure of fear and surrender to life.

The real rewards have been meeting these amazing, inspiring women. They have shared their true selves, flaws and all. They have held up the sword for all women to celebrate who they are right now. They have fearlessly told their extraordinary stories. We gave them pride and credence for being strong, and they gave us a moment of sisterhood.

We reserved the final page of this book for the fearless woman in your life. There's a place for a favorite photograph of her, and lines where you can write words that describe her special power to inspire. Maybe this fearless woman is your wife, mother, daughter, sister, or best friend. Maybe this woman is you.

For us, the real goal of midlife is to age *grate*fully: to be courageous instead of fearful, to be nurturing instead of critical, to use our power to create instead of destroy. Wrinkles and extra pounds need not get in the way of a remarkable, satisfying life. So, here's to the woman who is full of passion and life, has plenty to say, no longer cares what others think, loves the word *reinvention*, and is determined to make the world a better place—even if she can't find her car keys. Here's to fearless women everywhere!

LYNNE TWIST

LYNNE AT 20

This was taken when I was a bridesmaid at my friend's wedding. I remember thinking I had to get a tan to look good for that wedding and appear picture-perfect. Appearances were more important than reality then. As it happens, my husband turned out to be my prince, and fortunately I outgrew the concern about appearances.

LYNNE'S DECADES OF WORK as a fundraiser and environmental and humanitarian activist have taken her from executive workshops with some of the richest and most celebrated individuals in the world, to harsh environments in countries like Ethiopia, Bangladesh, India, and Guatemala, where deeply impoverished people labor under extreme subjugation and struggle simply to feed their families. Early in her career, Lynne's passion for making a difference led her to study with the visionary architect, engineer, and futurist Buckminster Fuller, then join him in a groundbreaking commitment to end world hunger. Lynne's role as the leading fundraiser for The Hunger Project engaged her in life-changing service and conversations with Mother Teresa, His Holiness the Dalai Lama, and other extraordinary leaders from around the globe.

Somewhere between saving the rain forest and empowering people, Lynne found time to write a book titled *The Soul of Money: Transforming Your Relationship with Money and Life*. Lynne's continued fearless dedication to changing the world demonstrates that we should never fear getting older—it just gives us more time to make a difference.

What has changed about your self-perception since you were a young woman?

I trust myself more. I know the dark time and the challenging time are actually the most fertile times for growth, just as seeds need to be planted in the dark earth before they can grow and flower.

If you could go back and speak to your younger self, what piece of wisdom would you share?

That the most powerful way to be is who you naturally are. The trap we fall into when we're younger is to try to be somebody or impress someone. That can be motivating, but it also leads us in directions that aren't authentically true to us, and from which we ultimately need to recover.

CATHERINE CURRY WILLIAMS

IN 1997, CATHERINE CURRY WILLIAMS LOST HER FIRST CHILD, Shane, to a degenerative nerve condition shortly after his birth. Her grief was overwhelming. But the pain of her loss was gradually channeled into a worthy cause as she began a project in Shane's memory. Had Shane lived, he would have spent his life in a wheelchair, so Catherine became a fearless advocate for children with disabilities. She, along with her husband and her best friend, headed up a team of volunteers to create Shane's Inspiration, a nonprofit organization dedicated to improving children's lives. For the past six years, her mission has been to develop universally accessible playgrounds, where children of all abilities can play together. Shane's Inspiration also provides community outreach and transportation programs for children with disabilities. Catherine is a valiant woman, an example of one who turned personal tragedy into a loving gesture that will continue to enhance the lives of families in the future.

What do you love most about being in the middle of your life?

Realizing that almost nothing is an emergency. I can take a deep breath or two and proceed with caution.

CATHERINE AT 23

That big smile on my face says I thought I knew everything. At forty-five, I realize I still have so much more to learn. Keeps me humble.

LINDA HANLEY

PROFESSIONAL ATHLETE, OLYMPIAN

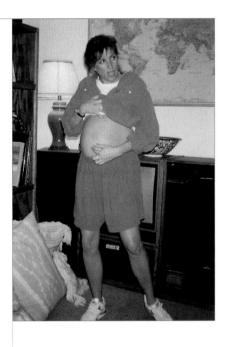

THE AVERAGE FORTY-FIVE-YEAR-OLD WOMAN might panic at the idea of putting on a bikini. Imagine how she might feel if she then had to stand among a group of women half her age—all in bikinis—and hurtle a volleyball across a net at a speed that defies returning it, every day, for a living. But then, Linda Hanley is no average woman. She may be one of the oldest women playing on the women's professional volleyball circuit, but she is also one of the best. "Nobody kicks butt like Linda," her younger teammates often say, aspiring to be as good as she is.

Linda knows she has gotten better with age, and having two children hasn't slowed her down. In fact, she feels it has made her a better athlete. Now she brings a finesse to her game that she never had in her younger days. And as far as looking good in a bikini? Judge for yourself.

What has changed about your self-perception since you were a young woman?

Midlife brings a calmness, you've settled in to who you are and can just enjoy the ride.

LINDA AT 30

Here I am pregnant with my first son. I thought that my career as a professional beach volleyball player would be over. Little did I know that the golden years were still ahead for me. In less than nine months I was playing again, and playing better than I ever had, and making more money than I ever dreamed of!

JONI MITCHELL

SONGWRITER, SINGER, MUSICIAN, POET, PAINTER

FEW WOMEN ALIVE TODAY HAVE the words *legend, icon,* and *genius* applied to them with little debate, but Joni Mitchell can wear each of these crowns. A revolutionary singer and songwriter, Joni has enjoyed a music career that has spanned four decades and yielded a collection of work considered by critics to be one of the best of her generation. It has also earned her induction into the Rock and Roll Hall of Fame (1997) and a Grammy for Lifetime Achievement (2002).

Canadian-born Joni came to America in the sixties, recording her debut album in 1968, but it was her 1969 album, the folksy *Clouds*—which featured her signature songs "Both Sides Now" and "Chelsea Morning"—that established her as a gifted writer. She soon became the universal voice of the disenchanted youth of that era with her socially conscious lyrics. "I used to think I could change the world," Joni muses. "I spent my youth worrying about it." She wrote the anthem "Woodstock" for the legendary music festival of that name, and "Big Yellow Taxi," a still-relevant song emblematic of a culture of consumption, is a popular cover for artists today. But perhaps what resonated most with women of our generation were her verses on love and its consequences. They were often reflections on her own romantic relationships with some of rock's leading musicians (David Crosby, Graham Nash, James Taylor), with whom she also collaborated artistically.

Over the course of thirty years, Joni's work has become impossible to classify, and she is now celebrated for her unique interpretations of music styles from folk to rock to jazz. Music-making has never been about commercial success for Joni. "I do it for myself, and sometimes I hit an illumination," she says.

What do you hate most about midlife but can laugh about anyway?

There is really nothing I hate about things now compared to the things I hated in my twenties. If you have had a full experiential life, if you live each phase of that life to the fullest, I don't think you get so stuck on this youth kick—you don't want to return there. Our culture has created such a fear of aging. This whole Viagra, facelift rat race— why do you want that? When you lose your hormones, it should be a time of freedom.

JONI AT 20

I had lived a lot of life when I was twenty. I wrote "Both Sides Now" when I was twenty-one, so I already knew love was an illusion. And like so many of our generation, I was raised on that fairy tale. We were all brainwashed into believing "my prince will come."

GLORIA ALLRED

GLORIA AT 23

In this photo, I was a single parent, about to embark on a career teaching in the public schools.

"FEARLESS" IS GLORIA ALLRED'S MIDDLE NAME. As an attorney with the high-profile Los Angeles firm Allred, Maroko & Goldberg, which she helped found, and with twenty-seven years of practice to her credit, she has dedicated her life to the betterment of humankind. She has won countless honors—including the President's Volunteer Action Award—for her pioneering legal work on behalf of women's rights and the rights of those who are discriminated against on account of their gender, race, age, sexual orientation, or physical condition. In addition, she founded and is currently serving as president of the Women's Equal Rights Legal Defense and Education Fund, which educates women about their legal, economic, social, and educational rights and assists them in vindicating those rights by providing access to the courts. She believes that she and millions of others have a duty to fight and end injustice against women. Now going strong at age sixty-three, Gloria continues to stand up, fearless, and give her undying support to women. When given the sword to hold in the photograph, Gloria quipped, "The sharpest sword we could have would be the passage of the Equal Rights Amendment, which we could use to win many legal battles for women."

If you could go back and speak to your younger self, what piece of wisdom would you share?

Don't believe in fairy tales. Most women are not going to get married and live happily ever after for the rest of their lives. Learn to take care of yourself, whether you are married or unmarried. Dependence can be dangerous to your physical, emotional, and financial health. Knowledge is power!

KARYN CALABRESE

KARYN AT 27

Here I am with my two young children. I was in a bad marriage, and it was one of the few times in my life when I didn't know what to do with myself. But I knew I was terrified of a life of being ordinary.

HOLISTIC HEALER, TEACHER, NUTRITIONAL COUNSELOR, RAW FOOD EXPERT

WITH FIERCE DETERMINATION, Karyn Calabrese knew she wanted to succeed in life. First, this former model was determined not to meet the same fate as her mother and grandmother, who died in their early fifties, younger than Karyn is now. Then she was determined to succeed as an African American woman who had suffered through a bad marriage and had two children to raise. So she took her passionate interest in health, diet, and lifestyle, turned it into a business, and became one of the most innovative leaders in the holistic health industry.

It all started with the purchase of a wheat-grass juicer, which eventually led Karyn to become a vegetarian and later a proponent of a raw food diet. She is the owner of the hugely successful raw food restaurant called Karyn's in Chicago as well as Karyn's Inner Beauty Center, a holistic therapy center that promotes healing the body naturally to correct damage done by unhealthy environments and poor food choices.

A sought-after speaker at community events and a former featured guest on the *Oprah Winfrey Show*, Karyn embodies the question she asks herself every morning: "If you don't take care of your body, the most magnificent machine you have ever been given, where are you going to live?" When asked for her feelings about being in midlife, she responded, "I'm not in midlife. This is just the beginning, I'm still young. If you live the kind of life I do, you'll live to at least 120."

If you could go back and speak to your younger self, what piece of wisdom would you share?

Never alter anything about yourself to make others comfortable. It empowers no one.

What has changed about your self-perception since you were a young woman?

In my youth I could never picture myself older than thirty—any years past that were useless. Now I see no ceiling on life goals, and youthfulness is infinite. At seventy I am going to become a concert pianist!

ERIN BROCKOVICH

ERIN AT 22

My early twenties were all about my babies. My identity was Mom. I didn't know anything else.

IT WOULD BE DIFFICULT TO FIND AN AMERICAN who doesn't know the name Erin Brockovich, thanks to the 2000 movie *Erin Brockovich,* in which Julia Roberts portrayed Erin (and for which Roberts won an Academy Award). But Erin is a woman who deserves the attention she receives. She consistently stands for what she believes in and tries to make a difference for people whose lives have been devastated. The movie tells the story of Erin's painstaking work on behalf of the citizens of Hinkley, California, whose groundwater had been contaminated by a toxin leaked from the nearby Pacific Gas and Electric Company's compressor station. In 1996, Erin and attorney Ed Masry spearheaded a direct-action lawsuit—the largest of its kind—against the giant utility company, and won the largest toxic-injury settlement in American history: $333 million in damages to more than six hundred Hinkley residents.

Erin grew up in Lawrence, Kansas, as the youngest daughter of an industrial engineer and a journalist. After graduating from high school in 1978, Erin earned an associate's degree from a business college in Dallas, Texas. Her first two marriages ended in divorce, leaving her with three children to raise alone. Today, happily remarried, Erin has become director of research at the firm Masry & Vititoe, one of the country's top motivational speakers, a television host, and the author of *Take It from Me: Life's a Struggle but You Can Win*, all while raising her children. Most important, she continues to spearhead major environmental lawsuits. She says she is just doing her job. We say she is the epitome of a fearless woman.

"I encourage everybody—when you go to bed—to do a check and balance of your morals, your values, and who you are," Erin says. "If I know of a harm to another person, I have to be the person that is called into action. I'm being true to myself, and at the end of the day we need to do that—listen to our hearts and follow our passions."

If you could go back and speak to your younger self, what piece of wisdom would you share?

I would probably tell myself and tell my kids as well that you can accomplish anything. But they wouldn't believe it. I wouldn't have. You have to learn that for yourself.

FRANCIE STEINWEDELL

FRANCIE AT 22

This is me in my early twenties. People saw me as beautiful, but I could not see any beauty. Everyone said I had Olympic talent, but I was lost and afraid. Underneath my so-called beauty and talent was undiagnosed depression. My self-medicating was the beginning of my long battle with addiction and alcoholism.

COMPETITIVE SHOW-JUMPING RIDER, HORSE TRAINER, COACH

FRANCIE STEINWEDELL BEGAN RIDING AT THE AGE OF FOUR, having inherited a love for horses from her mother, but her natural gifts as a rider proved to be much more than a childhood fancy. As a teen, she won some of the biggest national championships, such as the prestigious AHSA and ASPCA-Maclay Finals. She then became an international competitor in Grand Prix show-jumping, representing the United States in competitions from Falsterboro, Sweden, to Gijon, Spain. Yet guiding massive horses over jumps taller than most people at breakneck speeds isn't the only thing that makes this woman fearless. She believes her most courageous act was overcoming an addiction that haunted her most of her life. A perfectionist, Francie allowed every mistake made in the arena to stay with her long after the competition was over. This burden, and her attempt to numb it with drugs and alcohol, became what she considers to be the greatest obstacle in her life, far bigger than the hurdles that she physically faces astride her horses. "With each sober birthday I have, I look back with amazement and smile," she says. "I am very happy to have finally used my courage in such a positive way."

Francie still rides the animals she loves and wins blue ribbons against riders half her age in international competitions around the world. But her greatest pride comes from instilling mental strength in the young riders she now coaches, teaching them to put their emotion aside and rely on that inner strength in the arena. "My ability to be truthful to myself and own my past has helped me get to where I am today."

If you could go back and speak to your younger self, what piece of wisdom would you share?

I would tell her that she is worthy of the life she didn't think she deserved.

KATHY NAJIMY

ACTRESS, ACTIVIST, WRITER, DIRECTOR

KATHY NAJIMY HAS MADE A CAREER OF BEING clever, politically active, and versatile. You might know her from her one of her twenty-two films, including *Hocus Pocus* and *Sister Act* (she played Sister Mary Patrick) or as the voice of Peggy Hill on FOX's *King of the Hill*. You might recognize her as Olive from the NBC sitcom *Veronica's Closet*, or from her work on Broadway in *Dirty Blonde* and *Afterbirth: Kathy and Mo's Greatest Hits*, based on her award-winning HBO specials with Mo Gaffney. Kathy has also directed several off- and off-off-Broadway shows. But her true fearlessness comes out when she's touring the country speaking up for humanity. She's an activist for AIDS awareness, women's rights and equality, gay and lesbian rights, animal rights, and children's rights and well-being. She is a spokesperson for Project Angel Food, the Feminist Majority, Planned Parenthood, the Arab Anti-Discrimination League, and People for the Ethical Treatment of Animals (PETA). She's a fearless mother, too. Just ask her seven-year-old daughter.

KATHY AT 22

I used to think that I was
kind of a weirdo. Now
I have grown up and find
myself in a business
where all the fancy people
are simply ex-weirdos, too.

If you could go back and speak to your younger self, what piece of wisdom would you share?

I would warn myself that all the people who are "in charge," that I feel afraid of
or impressed by, are just regular schmos trying to make a buck and an impression
and are not that impressive. I would give myself the heads up to trust my taste
and my opinions and not think people with big jobs had big brains or big integrity.

Who or what had the biggest influence on how you view yourself?

Bette Midler, my dad, and Gloria Steinem. Maybe Ginger from *Gilligan's Island*.
Bette Midler convinced me you didn't have to look like a traditional starlet
to be famous, creative, and sexy. Gloria Steinem showed me I was not the only
feminist on the planet and that I wasn't insane for thinking girls/women
were superior. And my dad taught me that "you can be anything you want to be."

SISSY BOYD

SISSY AT 28

I took my body, such a unique
instrument of expression,
completely for granted.

WE NEVER KNOW WHAT LIFE HAS IN STORE FOR US. In youth we have a certain amount of confidence that our hopes and dreams will materialize. When life throws the hard stuff our way, we either get discouraged and stop playing or find our way through the pain to discover our fearless spirit.

At twenty, Sissy fled her narrow, suburban upbringing and entered the avant-garde scene of New York City. She was living her dream. Days, she studied dance at the Martha Graham School. Nights, she ran footloose and wild through all that the 1960s offered. There was no end to experimentation for a devoted bohemian: the Warhol scene, the Judson Church dance collective, films, and video art. She was at her prime—young, restless, daring, and beautiful. Life seemed glorious, with no doubt that it would continue so forever.

At the peak of her playfulness, Sissy—the dancer, the girl with a gift for movement—contracted a mysterious virus that completely paralyzed her. She couldn't even close her eyes. She was disillusioned and frightened. She had to relearn everything: movement, speech, expression. That's where the real work began. Sissy willed her muscles to move. She was finally able to close her eyes, and when she opened them again she began her long journey back to movement. She has persevered in her investigations, first through language, and now, at sixty, she is fearlessly dancing again.

She tells us, "I'm always looking for interesting parts in film and television. Parts for women who have aged and show their whole life in face and body." She continues to appear in producer Ken Roht's splendid dance extravaganzas. Her own work can be seen at The Evidence Room, a prestigious theater in Los Angeles, where she is a member.

What do you love most about being in the middle of your life?

Movement is my poetry, and no one appreciates even the slightest flow of motion more than I do now.

JOAN LUNDEN

JOAN AT 23

When I was younger, I think I perceived myself as much weaker and less capable. But the more I've dared to do and the more I've stepped up to opportunities and met challenges, the more I've realized how strong and fearless I really am. Here I am at twenty-three, new to the news biz and the streets of New York. I'm beginning my transformation to Fearless Woman.

JOAN LUNDEN, A RECOGNIZABLE FACE TO MILLIONS from her twenty-year stint as cohost of *Good Morning America*, is an unlikely pioneer. When Americans weren't used to seeing pregnant anchorwomen interviewing world leaders, she made that situation seem perfectly normal and natural. As *Good Morning America* cohost, she traveled the world to cover historic events, such as the fiftieth anniversaries of VE (Victory in Europe) Day and D-Day in Normandy, France; the 1984 and 1988 Winter Olympics in Sarajevo and Calgary, respectively; and the royal wedding of Charles and Diana in London. Joan has covered the inaugurations and administrations of Ronald Reagan, George H. W. Bush, and Bill Clinton. In a series of television specials, *Behind Closed Doors*, she takes viewers on journeys to places rarely if ever seen on television, such as behind the scenes at the CIA, in the sky in America's super-secret U-2 spy planes, and on board one of the most luxurious cruise ships in the world.

Now this eternally beautiful, wholesome woman is helping the public become familiar and comfortable with surrogate parenting. After becoming the mother of twins, carried by a surrogate mother, at the age of fifty-two, Joan is now expecting her second set of twins by the same surrogate. She has candidly shared her personal life with the public and has written four best-selling books, including her latest, *Growing Up Healthy*, to inspire and inform other women through her own experiences. She has been honored as Mother of the Year by the National Institute of Family Services, served as a national spokesperson for Mothers Against Drunk Driving, and hosted numerous television specials and series, including the award-winning *Mother's Day* on Lifetime TV. Joan is an inspiration for women who want to have it all—a happy family and career—without the unrealistic expectation of having it all at once.

What do you hate about being in midlife but can laugh about?

Gravity: While my confidence is defiantly higher, my ass is definitely lower.

IVANA CHUBBUCK

IVANA AT 20

In my early twenties, I
was a basket case. I wanted
to be an actress. Everything
was based on that desire.
I asked myself, Who am I?
What am I?

THE WORD "MUSE" IS BORROWED FROM THE MYTHS of ancient Greece, and the term describes one who inspires artists or poets. Ivana Chubbuck is the creative muse to some of the biggest names in Hollywood and, in midlife, is at the zenith of her creative power. The founder and director of the Ivana Chubbuck Studios, one of the foremost acting schools in the world, Ivana is the personal acting coach to superstars like Halle Berry, Charlize Theron, and Brad Pitt. Chubbuck's unique method of recreating human behavior, which is shared in her book *The Power of the Actor,* helps students tap into the depths of their own experience to achieve new levels of performance. This fearless woman helps her students face their deepest fears, re-create them, and ultimately draw upon them to bring a new character to life.

Life wasn't always so successful or glamorous for this determined woman. She began as a struggling actress, and her hard-won success has been earned over the course of many years. "I am fifty-one years old, and I've lived a lot of life, loved a lot of people," she says. "And I love that I am an accumulation of *all* those years."

If you could go back and speak to your younger self, what piece of wisdom would you share?

Grow up. It's all going to be quite different than you expected. Stop planning
and trying to micromanage everything. Let life happen. You think you know what
you need and want, but if you're open to the possibilities of life, it will be that
much more rewarding—spiritually and emotionally and, very often, financially.

LEEZA GIBBONS

LEEZA GIBBONS—THE NAME CONJURES UP AN IMAGE of a glamorous, blond television host, the front woman for *Entertainment Tonight* and the long-running daytime series *Leeza*. But today the role that is most important to her is that of wife, mother of three, and founder and board chair of her nonprofit foundation, the Leeza Gibbons Memory Foundation. After spending twenty-five years in the communications business, Leeza decided that the story of her mother's battle with Alzheimer's disease was the most important story ever entrusted to her care. She made a promise to her mom to tell that story and make it count. The manifestation of that promise is the foundation, formed in 2002, and its signature program, Leeza's Place: community centers where people with any type of memory disorder, as well as their caregivers, can go for education and support. Leeza says she hears her mom's voice in her head, "telling me to have helpful hands and a hopeful heart. I bring both to this enterprise, knowing that what we are doing is needed and will be such a resource for those families fumbling through the maze, numb with fear and loneliness." The glamour and beauty of Leeza Gibbons is still there in midlife, along with the courage and determination to tell a story that really does count.

Who or what had the biggest influence on how you view yourself?

Two words have defined how I view my life since I turned forty: *flexibility* and *forgiveness*. I still have high goals and expectations, but I no longer expect the script to play out just the way it is written in my head. That was preventing me from experiencing so many wonderful flukes. I don't waste my energy by holding grudges or hanging on to regrets. I am much more forgiving of myself and others. I count my blessings and not my stretch marks.

When did you realize you were courageous?

I don't think I really accepted my power as a woman until I realized that *no* was a complete sentence. When I stopped making excuses for saying it and began creating boundaries in my life, I knew real power.

LEEZA AT 20

At two decades into my maturation as a woman, I had no idea what was ahead. I felt powerful and full of possibilities, yet there was a tentative aspect to my expression of myself. I was in a hurry and painfully naive.

RHONDA BRITTEN

RHONDA AT 24

Partying. Dancing. Drinking.
My twenties were spent
looking for love in all the
wrong places. I looked happy
on the outside, but on the
inside, I was one lonely girl.

AUTHOR, LIFE COACH, TELEVISION PERSONALITY

RHONDA HAS BECOME FEARLESS WITH FORGIVENESS. When she was fourteen years old, on a cool and rainy Father's Day, her father shot and killed her mother and himself in front of her. The nightmare of being the only witness to this horrifying and life-changing event permeated every decision she subsequently made. After many years of pain, Rhonda didn't want to be around for midlife. Her mother never made it to forty, so she tried not to reach that age, either. Then, on the twentieth anniversary of the tragedy, she reached an amazing turning point. Calling upon her adult strength and wisdom, she decided that the past was no longer going to dictate her existence, and she courageously began to live her life with forgiveness.

As her personal healing began to take hold, Rhonda decided to use her growth to help other women, so she studied to become a life coach, trainer, and seminar leader. She started by coaching individuals and facilitating grief groups. In 2001, she became a best-selling author with her book *Fearless Living: Live Without Excuses and Love Without Regret.* Other books followed, including *Fearless Loving* and *Change Your Life in 30 Days.* Rhonda has an incredible passion for empowerment and can be seen as a life coach guiding participants on the popular NBC show *Starting Over*—a daily reality series in which women move into a house together to work out personal problems.

If you could go back and speak to your younger self, what piece of wisdom would you share?

There is nothing wrong with you. I wish that I could speak to every woman and whisper that phrase into her ear.

What do you hate about being in midlife but can laugh about anyway?

Sagging. Sagging butt, sagging arms, sagging chin. When I was twenty, I didn't think much about my body and it worked and looked great. Now, all my free time is spent taking care of my body, and working it out just to fight the sagging. And let's face it, the sagging is still winning.

MARILYN TAM

MARILYN AT 29

It was my wedding day. I was sitting in my apartment after our wedding and before the big dinner party with the photographer and immediate family hovering around. My husband was always close by me, beaming from ear to ear. We were moving back to the United States in a month after living overseas. It was a time of new beginnings, big transitions, and endless possibilities. Little did I know that less than nine years later he would be dead, killed by a sudden heart attack while mountain biking.

MARILYN TAM ARRIVED IN THE UNITED STATES in 1969 with two suitcases. A young immigrant from Hong Kong, she relied on her fearlessness to come halfway across the world alone and integrate herself into a foreign school system, beginning with a college education at the University of Oregon and then Oregon State University, where she received a bachelor's degree in Foods and a master's in Economics.

Marilyn's business career began as she climbed the corporate ladder at May Department Stores, a company that believed, as did she, in the importance of making a difference in the community. Her courage followed her as she grew in personal power and became, in rapid succession, the CEO of Aveda, the vice president of Nike, the president of Reebok, and the 1994 recipient of the Reebok Human Rights Award. Marilyn is the founder and executive director of the Us Foundation, which facilitates global action plans and dialogue to address social, economic, and environmental issues. She believes that philanthropy provides an essential balance and relevance to her life. She sees her recent book, *How to Use What You've Got to Get What You Want,* as a way to share with others the stories, principles, and actions that transformed her from an unwanted girl in Hong Kong to an international business leader, a philanthropist, and, most important, a generous person at peace with herself.

"I didn't know that I was courageous because I was just focused on my mission of making a positive difference in the world," she says modestly. "I didn't realize I was courageous even as I made my way through the corporate structure to run Fortune 500 companies. But it's my courage and my belief in Spirit that, in retrospect, sustained and fortified me to be who I am today and every day." In her photograph, the sword represents fotitude and the rose represents her connection with nature and Spirit—a sense of resolution and trust in something bigger that guides us and motivates us to be all that we can be.

If you could go back and speak to your younger self, what piece of wisdom would you share?

Live life each day! Don't worry so much and take things so seriously. Tomorrow may never come.

VICTORIA ROWELL

VICTORIA IN HER 20s

Dancing was the rudder
in my life. Foster care
was a calm lake and violent
ocean all in one.

DANCER, ACTRESS, MOTHER, ELEGANT WOMAN: To many, Victoria is best known for her role opposite Dick Van Dyke in *Diagnosis Murder* or in the Emmy Award–winning soap opera *The Young and the Restless.* Victoria has also starred in television and film roles opposite Bill Cosby, Will Smith, Beau Bridges, Samuel Jackson, and Jim Carrey. She has even danced with the American Ballet Theatre. But to the beneficiaries of her charity, the Rowell Foster Children's Positive Plan, which awards fine arts and academic scholarships to foster youth, she is just Vicki, a woman who cares.

Victoria is one of the country's leading champions for foster children. Placed into foster care herself at sixteen days old, Victoria found a loving connection with one of her foster mothers, Agatha Wooten Armstead. Because not every child in the foster-care system experiences positive mentoring, the successful actress decided to advocate on behalf of foster children, starting her charity and becoming the national spokesperson for the Annie E. Casey Foundation and Casey Family Services, established by visionary James Casey, the founder of United Parcel Service. "To survive eighteen years of foster care, and make it the cornerstone of my life, is the miracle," she says. Victoria fearlessly helps to give foster children choices and voices through art, higher education, fundamental health care, and jobs. She believes that there are so many opportunities still to come in the second half of her life, and she intends to use them to make a difference in the lives of children.

What has changed about your self-perception since you were a young woman?

Femininity + Intelligence = Power!

VICKI VYENIELLO

TEACHER, VICE-PRINCIPAL, TEACHER EDUCATOR

VICKI AT 21

That was me in 1970. I
thought I had it all planned
out. I was getting married,
moving into a new house, and
getting ready to work as
a first-grade teacher. I was
going to have two children,
then after the kids were
in school, I would go back to
teaching. Everybody said I
looked like Ali McGraw
then. Little did I know how
much my life would mirror
that of the character
she played in *Love Story*.

SOON AFTER SHE GOT MARRIED, Vicki thought she might be pregnant. Her abdomen was distended, and she had missed a few periods. Her visit to the doctor turned into a hospital nightmare when she found out she needed to have surgery to remove a cancerous tumor the size of a baseball. Months of radiation followed. No one expected her to live.

Vicki never had the two kids she dreamed of, but she has enlightened and encouraged other people's children for more than thirty years. They all have been her babies! Underpaid and underappreciated, Vicki is one of the millions of dedicated and creative people who show our children the path to education, morality, and self-expression, and she does this every day regardless of her personal hardships. Vicki is a perfect example of a fearless woman who nurtures others despite her own pain. She has influenced and comforted more than a thousand six-year-old souls in Room 1 for three decades while battling ovarian cancer and enduring the loss of her husband and her parents. As Vicki approaches retirement with abandon and pride, she is excited to see what the next half of her life will bring.

If you could go back and speak to your younger self, what piece of wisdom would you share?

Don't be afraid to stand out from the crowd. Allow yourself to experience
life more deeply so that you individuate yourself more quickly from the crowd.

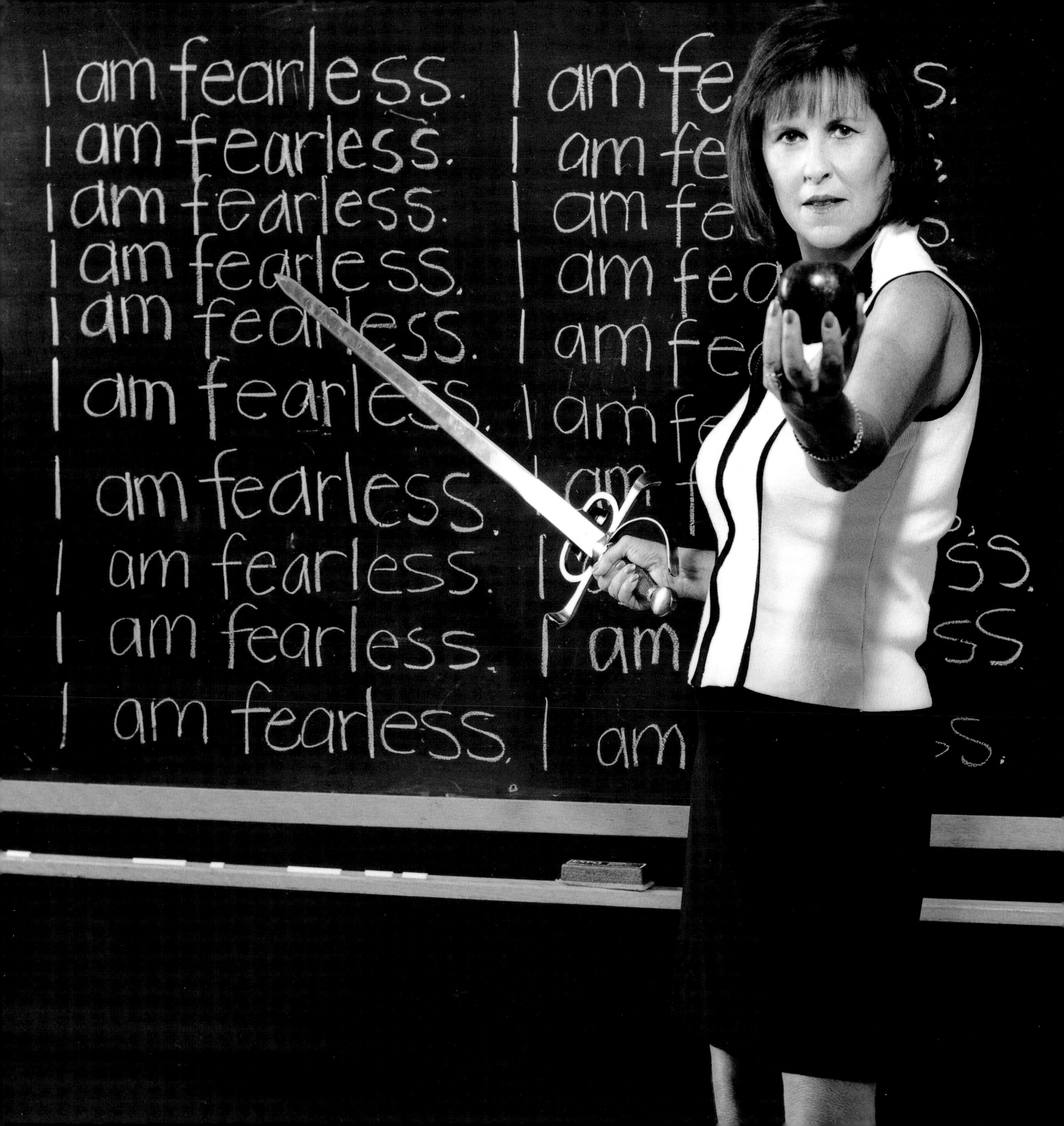

CHARLENE SPRETNAK

CHARLENE AT 29

When this picture was taken, I didn't know I was being photographed. I was at a small gathering of women and was listening to someone tell a story about her life, a deep and beautiful story.

AUTHOR, ACTIVIST, PROFESSOR OF PHILOSOPHY AND RELIGION

CHARLENE SPRETNAK HAS CONTINUALLY CHALLENGED THE STATUS QUO—from her groundbreaking work in the Women's Spirituality movement in the 1970s, to her cofounding of the Green Party movement in the United States in the 1980s, to her work on the community-based counterforce to economic globalization in the 1990s, to her recent effort to change the course of the Roman Catholic Church. In Charlene's first book, *Lost Goddesses of Early Greece*, she challenged the pre-Olympian myths of Greece. She then saw that the emergent Women's Spirituality movement was widely misunderstood, so she proposed a framework for it in an anthology titled *The Politics of Women's Spirituality*. She also wrote *Green Politics* and *The Spiritual Dimension of Green Politics*.

Her latest challenge has been to speak out against the Catholic Church's elimination of the traditional celestial power of the Virgin Mary when it modernized itself at Vatican II. In *Missing Mary: The Queen of Heaven and Her Re-Emergence in the Modern Church*, Charlene interprets and contributes to the contemporary resurgence of Marian spirituality. In her next project, she will challenge the general denial in art history of the influence of spirituality on many of the great modern artists. Charlene sees clearly and writes beautifully about her insights. This fearless intellectual is a great example of how the word can be more powerful than the sword. In her portrait, the sword serves as a shelf to support and honor Mary, the Queen of Peace, the Seat of Wisdom, the Mystical Rose.

What do you love most about being in the middle of your life?

This is a great time of life. I'm definitely feeling a burst of what Margaret Mead labeled "post-menopausal zest"! Not only am I drawn forward with enthusiasm for projects that I find fascinating, but I can feel satisfaction in seeing the success of so many movements and projects that I helped come into being thirty years ago. Our efforts have come to fruition, and the world is a better place for it. I feel fortunate to have been able to contribute.

LONNIE ALI

In my early twenties, I pretty much trusted everyone, was completely independent in thought, and perceived myself as totally capable of achieving any goal I set. When I married Muhammad in my late twenties, I thought I would retire to some quiet space in his shadow, and my new mission in life would be to keep the home fires burning.

IT'S SAID THAT BEHIND EVERY GREAT MAN IS A GREAT WOMAN, and Lonnie Ali is the strength behind one of the most recognized faces in the world. She fearlessly supports, nurtures, and manages the affairs of her beloved husband, Muhammad Ali, the three-time heavyweight boxing champion and world humanitarian who also happens to suffer from Parkinson's Disease.

Muhammad has used his celebrity for charitable causes at home and abroad—he's currently an ambassador of peace for the United Nations—and Lonnie has coordinated these efforts by running his business office and being the strength behind him. With a masters in business administration from UCLA and plenty of determination, she's well qualified for the job. Lonnie married Muhammad in 1986, aware of his medical condition and knowing that she would have to take over his business affairs and keep his health on track.

Lonnie has known Muhammad since she was six years old—before his first fight with Sonny Liston, when his name was still Cassius Clay—having grown up across the street from his parents in the suburbs of Louisville, Kentucky. Now, she clocks more than a hundred days a year with him in world travel. In addition, she's a full-time mother to their teenage son and serves on the boards of several health and humanitarian organizations like the Michael J. Fox Foundation for Parkinson's Research and the Lake Michigan College Foundation. She's also instrumental in development and fund-raising for the Muhammad Ali Museum and Education Center in Louisville, Kentucky, which strives to promote respect and understanding among different peoples, communities, and nations, and to inspire adults and children everywhere to be as great as they can be. Lonnie feels privileged to support Muhammad and these humanitarian causes, and he is fortunate to have a foundation as rock-solid as she.

If you could go back and speak to your younger self, what piece of wisdom would you share?

Listen more than you speak. Always try to be an advocate, not an adversary.

CCH POUNDER

ACTRESS, ACTIVIST

CCH POUNDER HAS ALWAYS BEEN A DETERMINED SOUL, which is evident in the diversity of her acting roles and her activism. She is also a warm, inviting, and very funny woman. CC was raised on a sugarcane estate in Guyana—each day she took a taxi, then a boat, and finally a bus to school. She received her higher education in Sussex, England. She has two evident passions. Acting is one: You might recognize her from the critically acclaimed FX series *The Shield* or from her role as Dr. Angela Hicks on the NBC series *ER* or from the role that first gained her recognition for her acting skills in the film *Bagdad Cafe.* She's been in countless movies and television shows, and, in the middle of her life, her acting career is not slowing down one bit. At fifty-one, she sees herself as being at the top of her game.

It's that kind of fearless attitude—and her activist spirit—that makes her such a good role model. CC's other passion took root in 1989, when she helped found the organization Artists for a New South Africa, which is dedicated to combating the AIDS pandemic and advancing democracy and equality in South Africa. And in a separate endeavor, she and her husband have built the Boribana Museum in Dakar, Senegal, the first contemporary art museum in the region. "There is nothing impossible that someone who believes enough in themselves cannot conquer," says CC. "And my journey is never-ending."

What has changed about your self-perception since you were a young woman?

I like me.

What do you hate about being in midlife but can laugh about?

My memory. There are two compartments: One is the rote memory, which is just fine. I can memorize and keep it with no problem. But don't ask me where my car keys are, because most of the time I have no idea.

CC AT 29

At the time this picture was taken, I was starving and unemployed. It was the middle of the day, and I was in a bar with a drink and a cigarette because I had nothing to do. This is when it all began. Now I'm doing exactly what I want to be doing, and I don't have to answer to anyone else's fantasy of the "making it" scenario.

ANGIE BUNCH

DANCER, TEACHER, DANCE COMPANY FOUNDER

AS FOUNDER AND PRESIDENT of Culture Shock Dance Troupes, Inc., a nonprofit professional hip-hop dance company and youth outreach organization, Angie Bunch is on the cutting edge of an art form usually associated with the very hip and the very young. Since its beginning in 1993 in San Diego, Culture Shock has grown into a national and international phenomenon, with troupes in Los Angeles, Oakland, Las Vegas, Chicago, Atlanta, Washington, D.C., and New York City, as well as Canada, France, Italy, Switzerland, Portugal, and the United Kingdom. In the 1980s, Angie realized that hip-hop—a form of funky urban dance that originated in the streets, much like rap music—had the power to transform the lives of inner-city kids, even though it was then regarded as just an urban street trend. While working as a Nike fitness athlete, representing the ultimate in physical fitness, she used the popular dance to reach out to teens and found it to be a positive outlet that kept them away from the drugs and violence prevalent in their communities. Out of this experience, she created her world-renowned dance troupe with a mission to cultivate self-worth, dignity, and respect for all people through music and dance.

Never one simply to get her toes wet, Angie dives headfirst into whatever challenges come her way—whether that's founding a dance company or having a baby after forty. "I put cart before horse in my life," she says. "There is always a tendency on my part to jump first and not to see any obstacles. I don't know how good that is, but I figure if I jump forward, I can always fall back!"

ANGIE AT 30

In this photo, I was just starting my fitness/dance career. I had already been dancing professionally for about eight years, mostly for Disney, so this was a whole new arena. I was just picked up by Nike, Inc., as a fitness/dance athlete and was feeling hopeful, nervous, and uncertain that I would have anything to offer.

What has changed most about your self-perception since you were a young woman?

I now know with certainty (something I never possessed before—what a luxury!) that I *am* on my path, that I *am* meant to be here, and that I *do* have value.

Who or what had the biggest influence on how you view yourself?

My daughter. Why I waited so long to have her is a mystery. I look in her eyes and see my worth.

BETH BRODERICK

BETH AT 30

That was the worst year of my life. One of my dearest friends, Lance Baker, succumbed to AIDS. I felt like a failure. I had spent my twenties working on behalf of persons with AIDS, and the disease continued to ravage the people around me. No matter what I did, it was never enough, I was never enough.

BETH BRODERICK IS A PHILANTHROPIC, tender woman who makes it her business to do everything she can to diminish the wrongs of the world. She never takes no for an answer. "I saw a bumper sticker the other day that defines my values," Beth explained. "It read: DIE TRYING. And so I shall."

Beth was only eighteen when she received her degree from the American Academy of Dramatic Arts in 1977—the youngest person ever to graduate from that school—and she moved to New York at nineteen. While struggling to begin her film career in the 1980s, Beth became aware of a strange and frightening occurrence among men in the gay community. Men were dying of a mysterious disease referred to then as "gay men's cancer." There was talk of quarantines, and violence toward gays escalated. Determined to help, Beth—along with several other early AIDS activists—founded the Momentum Project, a program that provides support for persons with AIDS in New York City. For Momentum, Beth learned to produce large-scale benefit galas, write grant proposals, and work with city government to procure food and resources. She has since used these skills to help other causes she cares about: the Los Angeles Mission's program for homeless women, the Good Shepherd Shelter for Battered Women and Their Children, the Hollygrove home for abused children, and El Proyecto del Barrio, which runs after-school programs, food banks, and other programs for immigrants.

Though Beth has experienced success in both movies and television—having played prominent roles in the TV series *Sabrina, the Teenage Witch*, *The Five Mrs. Buchanans*, and *Hearts Afire*, and the movies *The Bonfire of the Vanities, Shadowhunter, Fools Rush In, The Inner Circle,* and *State's Evidence*—her number-one goal has remained being a crusader for humanity. She feels that she has gained more than she could ever give in this service to her community. "I have met more than my share of heroes," she says. "I may not change the world, but I intend to die trying."

What do you hate the most about midlife?

The fact that women are taught to fear it.

LYN MASON & CAY LITCHFIELD

FEARLESS FRIENDS

WHAT HELPS ANY OF US TO BECOME FEARLESS? A good, solid friend. Lyn and Cay have been best friends since eighth grade, which adds up to forty-five years. They represent the strength we all receive from our lifelong female relationships. They have helped each other through catastrophic illnesses, losses of loved ones, and births of babies. Lyn and Cay lost each other for a few years while each got a divorce and started new lives, but not for very long. Like most of us, they found they missed the one person who really understands.

In midlife, their bond is as strong as ever. Despite years and miles, they continue to rely on the healing power of friendship to get them through the second half of life. What makes this friendship strong? "No secrets," says Lyn. "We're blatantly truthful and we make each other accountable." Their battle cry? "Together, we can do anything!" Good friends, like Cay and Lyn, bring out the courage in each other.

If you could go back and speak to your younger self, what piece of wisdom would you share?

Lyn: Don't look back.

What do you love most about being in the middle of your life?

Cay: I am free to be myself. I don't worry about what other people think anymore.

LYN AND CAY AT 16

Our high school had some strange rules on who could or could not go the prom, so we went together, as the men in our lives couldn't go with us. This played out in life many times.

SHOHREH AGHDASHLOO

SHOHREH AT 20

How do I describe myself at twenty? Like an army! I marched in everywhere, so determined! Even at this young age, I knew I was destined for something great.

OSCAR-NOMINATED ACTRESS Shohreh Aghdashloo is used to taking long journeys, both physical and metaphorical. Her physical journey began in 1979, when she found her acting workshop in Tehran, Iran, had been closed down by revolutionary guards. As she stood before the Drama Workshop, now walled up with cement and brick, the Iranian-born film and stage actress decided Tehran was no place for a liberated woman like herself. Escaping the tyranny of the Ayatollah Khomeini was the only thing this fearlessly independent woman felt she could do. She fled the country, driving for a month across Europe until she reached London and a new life. The Iranian press then banned mentions of her name. Ironically, her will to succeed has made her one of the most famous and admired women in her country today.

Her career journey—from a struggling actress to a 2003 Oscar nominee—was long as well, taking twenty-five years. The role of her lifetime came in playing Nadi, the Iranian wife of a proud immigrant in the movie *House of Sand and Fog*, based on the 1999 novel by Andre Dubus III. With that part, she made history by becoming the first Iranian or Middle Eastern actress to be nominated for an Academy Award for best supporting actress. Portraying Nadi was a dream come true for Shohreh, who had wanted to play the part since she'd read the book years before. Now living in Los Angeles, married to playwright Houshang Touzie, and the mother of a teenage daughter, Shohreh is inundated with scripts but only interested in making movies that enlighten as well as entertain. She has turned down many offers to play terrorists, fearlessly refusing to be stereotyped. But one thing Shohreh Aghdashloo wholeheartedly embraces is the belief that dreams really do come true—as long as you give them time.

If you could go back and speak to your younger self, what piece of wisdom would you share?

There is a saying I am very fond of: Age is a matter of mind. If you don't mind, it doesn't matter.

ANDREA RIDEOUT

ENTREPRENEUR, HANDYWOMAN, RADIO PERSONALITY

A FEARLESS WOMAN IN A MAN'S WORLD, Andrea Rideout sees no glass ceiling. From managing her high-school football team to owning a hardware manufacturing company to creating an eclectic mail-order hardware showroom, Andrea has competed in traditionally male realms with confidence and ease. As life will have it, Andrea has experienced a few setbacks that might have daunted someone less resilient. In 1991 a tornado nearly destroyed her successful hardware company. Pregnant with her third child, Andrea felt lost and depressed as she surveyed the ruins. Ready to give up, she saw that someone had written "When the going gets tough, the tough get going" on what was left of a blackboard. Andrea took this to heart, created a new and improved space, sold the business, and then began manufacturing her own line of vintage reproduction door hardware. Her new company, Nostalgic Warehouse, was one of only two women-owned hardware companies in the United States at the time. Andrea now hosts her own women's home-improvement radio show, *Ask Andrea*, and is a popular guest on TV shows around the country, encouraging other women to "do it yourself."

ANDREA AT 23

This was a time before I truly believed in my unique gifts. I had no clue that I even had gifts, and now— after a lot of trials—I appreciate my own special voice and perspective.

What has changed about your self-perception since you were a young woman?

I am more confident in my own opinion, and I am not afraid to look foolish if I am wrong. I am also much more understanding of other people.

Who or what had the biggest influence on how you view yourself?

A million failures and successes. They all add up to who I am today. I relish failure as much as success. It's the only way to learn.

KATHY ELDON

KATHY AT 20

This was the summer of 1967. I was heading to the Cedar Rapids Cotton Ball with a blind date. I felt plain and dumpy in a homemade dress and wore the shawl all night to cover my bulging hips. I couldn't wait to leave Iowa, join the Peace Corps, and change the world.

HOW DOES A MOTHER TURN A BRUTAL ACT OF VIOLENCE into a quest for world peace? Kathy Eldon fearlessly set an example when her twenty-two-year-old son, photojournalist Dan Eldon, was stoned to death in Somalia. While full recovery from a loss so horrifying may be impossible, Kathy and her daughter, Amy, have found a way to bring healing into their lives and make a difference in the world by dedicating their energy to promoting peace and tolerance. Kathy, a former journalist and author, has founded Creative Visions, a film and television production company dedicated to supporting "media that matters." Together, mother and daughter created a foundation to empower young people to use various media to influence positive change in the world, an endeavor partly funded by proceeds from exhibitions of Dan's stunning art journals. Kathy, who lectures around the world, has been featured on *Oprah* and on several television specials, including a recent *National Geographic* documentary about Dan and his legacy.

If you could go back and speak to your younger self, what piece of wisdom would you share?

This, too, shall pass.

What has changed about your self-perception since you were a young woman?

There was always so much to criticize about myself—my looks, behavior, my lack of achievements. Now, though I wish I could look better and do more, I appreciate each day, grateful simply to be alive and able to do what I love.

When did you realize you were courageous?

I have never felt particularly courageous. My parents taught me to stand up for what I believed, no matter what, and I have tried to live up to their example. Now I want to be bolder, noisier, and braver about important issues.

DONZALEIGH ABERNATHY

DONZALEIGH AT 19

Here I am at nineteen, as a student in Boston, studying acting even though I was extremely shy. I was passionate about dance— jazz, modern, and ballet— taking at least two dance classes a semester. I lived for the moment then, never giving much thought to fortune or the mysteries of life.

DONZALEIGH IS THE YOUNGEST DAUGHTER of the Reverend Ralph L. Abernathy, who, along with Martin Luther King Jr., fearlessly led the culture in standing up for civil rights. Influenced by these great gentlemen, she learned early on to face the challenges of injustice using the wisdom of nonviolence. Overcoming fear has been a part of her life from an early age. "When I was four, the Sixteenth Street Baptist Church [in Birmingham, Alabama] was bombed and those little girls were killed," she says. "I knew that could happen to us." She remembers praying that her family wouldn't be bombed while they were sleeping. She also remembers her father's words: "Fearlessness is when you are afraid and do it anyway. Courage is when you rise above your fear."

An accomplished actress, Donzaleigh is proud of her creative achievements and feels her life's work has been to become her own person, independent of her family. She is one of the stars of (and one of the few women in) the HBO motion picture *Gods and Monsters,* a Civil War drama in which she plays the only slave. Her other acting credits include *Don King: Only in America, Chicago Hope, Miss Evers' Boys, EZ Streets, Murder in Mississippi,* and a regular lead role in the Lifetime series *Any Day Now.* To honor the beloved men in her life, she wrote the book *Partners to History,* a tribute to the bravery and determination of these historical icons who influenced our nation with their peaceful courage. She is a founding member of New Road School, a K–12 private, independent school in Santa Monica, California, that promotes cultural, racial, and economic diversity.

Who or what had the biggest influence on how you view yourself?

My grandmother. She ran the most successful farm owned by a black person in the state of Alabama in the Forties. She was an Earth Mother. She taught homeopathy before anyone knew what it was. When I would go to the country to be with my grandmother, I would feel rich—rich with the land. She never raised her voice. She called my grandfather Sweet. I loved her feminine yet strong ways.

JOIE DAVIDOW

AUTHOR, MAGAZINE EDITOR, JOURNALIST, OPERA SINGER

JOIE DAVIDOW HAS ACHIEVED MUCH IN HER LIFE: an Ivy League education, a career as an opera singer, and another as a journalist and editor in the glamorous world of fashion. But it's recently, in midlife, that she feels she has realized her greatest accomplishment of all. Staying true to what she believes is her calling, she has written a memoir of great honesty and power that details her struggle to overcome a common deformity that affects millions of Americans: a port wine stain that covers the left side of her face. Joie fearlessly conveys this story in her book *Marked for Life*. "What I realized is that although I felt I was grotesque, inadequate, and different," she says, "my birthmark was simply a metaphor for all of us who feel that we are 'less than' and just not enough." Today she feels emancipated from the self-loathing that haunted her youth, and she serves as an example to women everywhere, proof that by learning to accept and love yourself, you can find lasting fulfillment.

What has changed about your self-perception since you were a young woman?

When I was younger, I never gave myself a break. I forgave my friends for all sorts of failures, but I forgave myself nothing. Over the decades I've learned to forgive myself for gaining weight, losing my car keys, or spending too much money on shoes, and to congratulate myself for being kind, generous, funny, and loving.

When did you realize you were courageous?

I always thought of myself as a gentle, shy woman who would never intentionally hurt anyone. But when I started *L.A. Style* magazine, I had to transform myself into a tough businessperson who took risks, said and did unpopular things when necessary, and demanded respect. In the early months of the project, I was nervous a lot of the time. Then one day, a colleague amazed me by saying she admired my fearlessness, and I realized I had made a transition. Women are held back so often by the fear that they'll be perceived as "hard." But at the time, I simply didn't have the luxury of worrying about that.

JOIE AT 28

No matter what I looked like, or what I achieved, it wasn't enough. My birthmark made me feel different, and that there was always going to be something that just wasn't right with me.

ANDREA THOMPSON

ANDREA AT 26

Here I am in the south of France, 1986. It was my honeymoon. My husband and I were having trouble already. He had displayed some reluctance or regret over marriage just after we had done the deed. Some time to think of it! I couldn't wait to get home. I thought I was too fat, always!

ACTRESS, JOURNALIST

MOST ACTRESSES DREAM OF LANDING A ROLE on the number-one prime-time television show and most, having landed it, hold on to it for as long as possible. But most actresses aren't like Andrea Thompson, who shocked the television world when she announced her departure from her critically acclaimed role as Detective Jill Kirkendall on *NYPD Blue* to become a journalist and news anchor in Albuquerque, New Mexico. She then worked for *CNN Headline News* and was the voice and face of *Court TV* for two years. Andrea is now working on an MBA and has never regretted any of her decisions; she feels that reinventing oneself is one of the most liberating things a woman can do.

"I know that in terms of popular media, women are considered less attractive as they grow older," she says. "But my female friends, my best friends, grow ever more alluring to me as they age. There is a wisdom, a freedom, a confident sexiness in a woman over the age of forty that no woman under forty can possibly duplicate—if you don't look backward or allow anyone else to define who you are. We are so much more than our youth or beauty."

And as our fearless cover girl emphatically explains, "Taking chances, leaping into the void, re-energizing one's goals—my hero is Madeleine Albright, who didn't make her personal leap into public service and the government sector until after her three daughters were grown and had left the nest. Then, she went on to become the first female Secretary of State for the United States of America. That's one kick-ass woman!"

Who or what had the biggest influence on how you view yourself?

My mother had the strongest, most enduring influence on how I view myself. She infused me with the belief that I could have or be or do anything I wanted. That the only person who could stop me was me. And that I should never allow anyone to define who or what I am.

What do you hate about being in midlife but can laugh about anyway?

That I'm dating a gorgeous, sensitive, kind, athletic surfer who happens to be only 21 but I'm embarrassed to go anywhere with him. Not embarrassed for me but for him!

LOIS LEE

LOIS AT 25

I was twenty-five years old in this photo, teaching a social research class at California State University, Dominguez Hills. It was the same year I initiated lawsuits against the Los Angeles Police Department for the unequal enforcement of prostitution laws.

CHILD WELFARE CRUSADER, ATTORNEY, FOUNDATION PRESIDENT

EVERYONE FROM LOIS LEE'S CHILDHOOD tells her that she was born to be a crusader. And what a formidable crusader she has become, as the primary force in the battle to protect and rescue our nation's children against the ravages of prostitution. Dr. Lee, who has her Ph.D. in sociology and anthropology, did her dissertation on "The Pimp and His Game." She gave up a promising career as a social researcher to pursue her dream of protecting those less fortunate. As the founder and president of Children of the Night, a drop-in center and home for children on the street, she has effectively kept 80 percent of the teens and children her organization assists from returning to a life of abuse and degradation. Dr. Lee trains police detectives in fighting child prostitution, and she fearlessly takes on the pimps and adults who exploit these children by confronting them in court as an expert witness. As if that weren't enough, she became an attorney so that she could fight these predators with the most effective of weapons—the law. The many honors she has been awarded include the President's Volunteer Action Award, which Ronald Reagan presented to her at the White House in 1984.

If you could go back and speak to your younger self, what piece of wisdom would you share?

You will never reach the top of the mountain because your life journey will bring you more welcome challenges and even more fulfillment day after day.

What do you hate about being in midlife but can laugh about anyway?

Midlife men.

JOAN CHEN

JOAN AT 24

This picture was shot on the set of *Tai-Pan* [in which she acted in 1986]. I had all the youth and physical beauty in the world, but I was deeply insecure and unhappy. The feeling of unworthiness was overwhelming because I had failed in my first love and could not recover from it.

ACTOR, WRITER, DIRECTOR

JOAN CHEN'S ACTING CAREER BEGAN in China in the mid-1970s when, at age fourteen, she was discovered by the wife of Mao Tse Tung at a Chinese rifle range and subsequently recommended to movie producers. Her 1980 performance in *Little Flower* earned her the Chinese equivalent of an Academy Award for best actress. She moved on to work in America, where audiences know her best for her roles in the movie *The Last Emperor* (1987) and the television series *Twin Peaks* (1990). But her most courageous work began in 1998, when she returned to her homeland to cowrite and direct the critically acclaimed and politically volatile movie *Xiu Xiu: The Sent Down Girl*, a condemnation of the Communist 1970s cultural revolution as seen through the eyes of a teenage girl.

This account of the "sent down" policy, in which young people's lives were devastated when forced to leave their families and do trade work for the Communist Chinese government, was something that Joan witnessed firsthand as a child. When the Film Bureau, which approves films for the Chinese public, proposed changes that Joan felt would have undermined the script, she decided to work without an official permit. With a crew of sixty she headed to remote parts of the Sichuan province and the Tibetan borderland, where she convinced local officials she'd made proper arrangements. As a precaution, she had each day's footage smuggled out of the area. High altitude, limited food supplies, and primitive plumbing were nothing compared to the constant dread of being discovered and having her work destroyed. Fearlessly, she moved forward. Her completed picture, banned in China, became a hit at both American and European festivals and in Taiwan, where it swept the Golden Horses (the Taipei equivalent of the Oscars). Now living in San Francisco with her husband, Joan professes, "Courage is going ahead even without expecting to win."

What has changed about your self-perception since you were a young woman?

The free-floating angst of my younger days is gone. With young children and aging parents to care for, there is a stronger sense of duty and responsibility, which makes me feel more deeply rooted in life.

JUDY WEIDER

JUDY AT 27

Growing up I hated my
curly hair. Then Angela Davis
freed me [a reference
to the Sixties' black feminist
activist with the huge Afro].

IT CAN BE HARD TO SEE OPTIONS when one feels like an outsider, especially for a lesbian woman striving to make an impact in the world of journalism, but Judy Weider has chosen to use that perspective as an asset. As the first female editor-in-chief for the gay and lesbian community's biggest periodical, *The Advocate*, she is a perfect representation of a woman comfortable in midlife. Grateful for the lessons of the past decades and ready to take on the years ahead, Judy has embraced her life with courage and compassion.

Judy got her big journalism break in 1971, when she became the founding editor of *Right ON!*, the first black teen magazine. In a career with many twists and turns, she went on to become a songwriter for the Supremes and then a freelance music journalist, following such heavy-metal bands as Guns N' Roses, Iron Maiden, Poison, and Judas Priest on their European tours. Once a closeted lesbian, she faced her many obstacles fearlessly, with grace and tact. When working with born-again Christians in the Motown world— people who had no tolerance for anything gay—she responded with patience, focusing on the beauty and creativity of her colleagues instead of taking their perspectives personally. And in the overindulged, womanizing rock-star realm, where the best way for a woman to get a juicy story was to sleep with the band, Judy instead used her wit, intelligence, and charm to get the scoop—traits she has called upon throughout her life.

Today, Judy is the senior vice president of LPI Media, the company that owns *The Advocate, Out, The Out Traveler, HIV Plus*, and Alyson Books. As the editorial manager of these award-winning publications, Judy's renegade spirit is now spreading the wonders of individuality to the world. Still, she is looking ahead much more, toward a gay family magazine and a television partnership, further proving that life remains an adventure and a challenge.

Who or what had the biggest influence on how you view yourself?

Bob Dylan. He taught me that it is possible to say something compelling and odd and make a difference and be amazing.

Melissa Manchester

MELISSA AT 28

I was in my late twenties.
During that period, I wrote,
recorded, and toured a
lot—one new album every
year for years. I rarely
felt like I could be "heard"—
by management, sound
technicians, producers. I
hadn't found a way to make
my needs clear. I hadn't
yet connected with caring for
my body through nutrition
or exercise, and my hair
always had a mind of its own.

A WELL-KNOWN SINGER/SONGWRITER of the seventies and eighties, Melissa Manchester is fearless about being authentic. At fifty-three, she refuses to let the latest craze of young, blond, undulating female pop stars keep her from believing she has a purpose, a message, a voice, and insights that plenty of others can relate to. Even after a ten-year hiatus from the music industry, she believes that singing and writing are what she's been put on earth to do.

Melissa began her music career at fifteen as a successful jingle singer—an unlikely start for a woman who now sings from the heart. In the late seventies, she performed with Bette Midler—as one of the original backup singers called the Harlettes. After struggling for many years to get her own work recognized, she eventually secured a record deal and went on to record classic hits like "Midnight Blue," "Don't Cry Out Loud," "Come In from the Rain," "Whenever I Call You Friend," and "You Should Hear How She Talks About You."

Once her son, Nathan, and daughter, Hannah, came into her world, however, Melissa devoted her energy to her family, taking time off from recording and touring to focus on motherhood. But recently, an urge to express her creativity has enticed her into writing once more, and in 2004 she released her first original album in ten years: *When I Look Down That Road*. It was fearlessness that allowed her to take that long break from recording and fearlessness that prepared her for a return. No age barrier is going stop this talented musician from connecting to others; she's living proof that music transcends age and time.

Who or what had the biggest influence on how you view yourself?

The biggest influences on my life have been my kids being born; being loved so deeply by my husband; my mother, Ruth, for her shining example of fabulousness; my sister, Claudia, for our deepening friendship; and Judy Garland, Ella Fitzgerald, and Eleanor Roosevelt for their impeccable commitment to greatness. Columbine and 9/11 reinforced to me how important songs could be to clarify anguish and underscore what is precious in life.

JEANIE LINDERS

JEANIE AT 26

In this photo I was taking on life as a celebration—or so I thought at the time. I love the freedom of this photo and of the path my life has taken.

CREATOR OF "MENOPAUSE: THE MUSICAL"

JEANIE LINDERS HAS TAKEN MENOPAUSE "flash by flash" and playfully presented it to a sisterhood of twenty-first-century women. They come in droves from all over the nation to openly laugh at, commiserate about, and appreciate her popular show *Menopause: The Musical*—a song-filled stage production about four midlife women who meet in Bloomingdale's and bellow parodies about hot flashes and waning hormones. What began as a modest little play in Orlando, Florida, is now playing to full houses in Chicago, New York, Boston, Los Angeles, and many other U.S. cities. Soon it will be moving to the global stage in Australia, the United Kingdom, and Southeast Asia. Jeanie has not merely put smiles on midlife women's faces; she has given us a sense of community. A far cry from the "silent passage" that menopause used to be, Jeanie's bold celebration of women and "the change" gives a message that is loud and clear: We are not alone!

Reinvention is what keeps Jeanie young, as her diverse work history illustrates. For ten years, she was president and CEO of an advertising agency that specialized in entertainment and hospitality accounts. She's also been a high-school teacher, a public-relations road manager, and an arts and development consultant, and she is the author of *Womankind,* a book of poetry for and about women. She appears to have the energy of three. With a little smile on her face, she eloquently delivers her beatitude: "Cursed are they who live to exist yet fail to live while existing, for theirs is the sin of satisfaction."

What has changed about your self-perception since you were a young woman?

At this stage of the game, I know that I know. Before, I just hoped that I knew.

BROOKE MEDICINE EAGLE

BROOKE MEDICINE EAGLE IS A NATIVE AMERICAN *metis,* or medicine woman. "It means finding your path, waking up to your true gifts," she explains, "and using them for the healing of the planet." Born on the Crow reservation in Montana, she became aware of her fearlessness at the age of four, when she watched her alcoholic father beat her mother. She then did what no one else was able to accomplish: Standing between her parents, she made her father stop. It made her feel like she alone was responsible for protecting her mother, a burden she carried until she almost perished in a fire at the age of eight. "My soul in some ways caused that to happen," she says, "because the fire burned up my anger at my father." During Brooke's recovery time in the hospital, her mother found the courage to leave her husband. She then sent Brooke away from the reservation in hopes of assimilating her into the white culture.

Brooke later attended the University of Denver, earning degrees in psychology and mathematics. But she was led back to the reservation in 1973 after a conversation with her father, ironically, who suggested she pursue her spiritual yearnings by studying with a medicine woman named Stands Near the Fire. This was the first of many teachers with whom Brooke would study, but when she found some of the male elders from traditional cultures expected sexual favors in return for their knowledge, she refused and fearlessly exposed them. She has since found her true path, attaining spiritual knowledge as a woman and not as an elder. She feels she is only halfway on the path to the full flowering of her life and believes she will live until 120. She leads retreats and ceremonies internationally and conducts wilderness camps at her childhood home ranch, Sacred Ground, in the Flathead Valley of Montana. She has also written two books, *Buffalo Woman Comes Singing* and *The Last Ghost Dance*, and produced a CD of spiritual music called *Gathering: The Sacred Breath*.

BROOKE AT 35

I've lost track of early photos, so this one at thirty-five seems young! I'm relaxing before conducting a ceremony in the high country, and I don't feel that much different now.

If you could go back and speak to your younger self, what piece of wisdom would you share?

Whatever you vibrate, you create! So, as soon as you can in your life, get help to clear the traumas, irrational fears, angers, and other negative "vibrations" from your life and body. Everything will unfold more easily in your life for having done so.

SHERRY WILLIAMS

SHERRY AT 23

I was in my mid-twenties, living my dream, but not smart enough to know it. I was working at a craft I totally loved, but I was also totally self-absorbed.

JAZZ SINGER, RECORDING ARTIST

SHE LEARNED THE JOY OF MUSIC FROM HER FATHER, listening to the music of Count Basie that "just called out my name." But even though Sherry Williams started singing as a six-year-old and began performing professionally at eighteen, she was discouraged from following her bliss because singing for money was something that "good girls" didn't do. Yet she believed in her talent and found a way to support herself with it. At forty-seven, the jazz singer recorded her first solo CD, *The Way You Love Me*, and since turning fifty she has recorded three more. Sherry believes she is a channel for her gift; all she has to do is get out of her own way and let the passion run through her. She calls upon her fearlessness to book herself into clubs around the country and record her music without the accolades and financial rewards showered upon superstars. Explaining why she stays so focused, this elegant woman explains, "Because I do what I want to do. I live my passion, what I want to do with my life, not what someone thinks I should be doing with it. I don't think of it as fearlessness, I just think it's necessary."

If you could go back and speak to your younger self, what piece of wisdom would you share?

Think! You are brilliant—use it wisely.

What has changed about your self-perception since you were a young woman?

Now I know I'm brilliant. Better use it wisely.

Jackie Kallen

JACKIE AT 24

When I was in my twenties, I lacked the confidence and pride that I have today. I was always afraid of doing or saying the wrong thing. Now I know that it doesn't matter. Whatever I say and whatever I do is the right thing—for me.

BOXING MANAGER, AUTHOR, MOTIVATIONAL SPEAKER

JACKIE KALLEN IS A FIGHTER OF HER OWN KIND. After a ten-year career as a publicist for world boxing champion Thomas Hearns and the legendary Kronk Boxing Team in Detroit, Jackie felt that she knew enough to find a boxer of her own and turn him into a world champion. As one of the only women ever to take on the boxing arena as a manager, Jackie helped lead James Toney and three other boxers to world championships. Her story inspired the movie *Against the Ropes,* in which her character was played by Meg Ryan. Although Jackie's walls are covered with awards and honors and she has served as the commissioner of the International Female Boxing Association and been nominated twice for the Manager of the Year award by the Boxing Federation, she admits that she continues to battle both sexism and discrimination in the traditionally male realm of boxing.

But it's not all about competing in a man's world for Jackie. An important part of her life's work is to travel around the country to raise awareness about women's health issues—Jackie herself lives with coronary artery disease and osteoporosis and has had two breast lumpectomies. She is also active in several Los Angeles charities, including women's shelters, and is the author of *Hit Me with Your Best Shot: A Fight Plan for Dealing with All of Life's Hard Knocks.* She currently manages several boxers and can be seen on the NBC reality series *The Contender,* where she is "den mother" and gym manager to the boxers.

What has changed about your self-perception since you were a young woman?

I know now that I am good just the way I am—plus or minus a few pounds or wrinkles. It's the person I am on the inside that matters. The rest is just gift-wrapping. It's always what's inside the box that counts.

SHARI BELAFONTE

SHARI AT 23

I wanted to be a director of photography, a technical director, and/or a producer. I had just graduated from Carnegie-Mellon Institute, with a BFA in drama production—not acting. I always had a camera with me; I dressed like a guy, walked like a guy, acted like a guy, and just plain wanted to be accepted as one of the guys.

PHOTOGRAPHER, FILMMAKER, ACTRESS, MODEL

SHARI BELAFONTE, DAUGHTER OF SINGING SUPERSTAR HARRY BELAFONTE, was born with the kind of natural beauty that makes people stop and take notice. But rather than use her looks to get in front of the camera, she always intended to work behind it. At the age of nineteen, on a fluke, she sent her picture to a few modeling agencies, thinking modeling might be a lucrative way to make money in her spare time. She was, she recalls, "floored" when the top agency in Los Angeles called her the day after they received her pictures and then signed her soon after. Modeling for such high-profile accounts as Calvin Klein led to acting on TV series like *Hotel*. Yet ultimately, in midlife, acting led her back to her original passions, photography and filmmaking. While hosting an Internet adventure travel show in Costa Rica, she started photographing the terrain and wildlife. She then shot all the promotional photos for PBS television's thirteen-part series *Travels in Mexico and the Caribbean with Shari Belafonte*, which she also hosted. She's recently finished directing photography for the feature film *Betty's Treats* and will soon shoot and direct her first country music video.

Shari has fearlessly traded Hollywood artifice—the hair extensions, makeup, and sexy clothes—for jeans, combat boots, and flannel shirts. In a business that emphasizes physical perfection and youth, she is a fearlessly aging rebel. Her natural beauty shines, and she is at ease with herself. "When I was an actress, publicists used to lie about my age in press releases, making me younger," she recalls. "Now it doesn't matter if I'm fifty, because I am behind the scenes. And besides, I never have had a problem with getting older. I love being fifty!"

What has changed about your self-perception since you were a young woman?

I always forget that I'm fifty, so I still do things that I did when I was in my twenties. Of course, I'm a little stiffer now, so I don't do them quite as quickly.

What do you hate about being in midlife but can laugh about anyway?

I used to have killer six-pack abs. Now, I've got a keg!

DIANA NYAD

DISTANCE SWIMMER, JOURNALIST, TELEVISION HOST, REPORTER

IMAGINE SWIMMING FOR TWO DAYS STRAIGHT, sharks and jellyfish your constant companions, in choppy, dangerous waters. No, this isn't the premise of the latest reality TV show; it's the remarkable and true story of distance swimmer Diana Nyad. In 1979, Diana stroked her way to the longest swim in history—102.5 miles, from the island of Bimini, in the Bahamas, to the Florida shore—and her record still stands. In the ten years leading up to that swim, Diana broke numerous world records and earned many honors, among them a place in the National Women's Sports Hall of Fame.

Diana ended her swimming career on that note, but her adventures are far from over. She's enjoyed a long career in television reporting and writing, working as an announcer with ABC's *Wide World of Sports*, a senior correspondent for Fox Sports News, and a host on National Public Radio.

Yet the work Diana is most proud of is with World T.E.A.M. Sports, an organization that teams able-bodied and disabled athletes for unique sporting adventures around the world. For the 1998 Vietnam challenge, Diana joined a team of cyclists—which included veterans from both sides of the Vietnam War—for a 1,200 mile journey from Hanoi to Ho Chi Minh City. It was, perhaps, the biggest step toward full reconciliation between Americans and Vietnamese since the Vietnam War and a poignant gesture of peace.

But for Diana, the rewards she seeks are far beyond physical. "Today," she says, "accomplishments that I value are being a true friend, being a progressive member of my community, and leading my circle of colleagues toward peace and loving communication."

When did you realize you were courageous?

I've always had courage. Whether I was an oblivious twenty-something or a kinder, gentler fifty-something, I've never been meek. I got the sense very early in life that this life is desperately precious and equally short. I've always had the courage to live every waking hour with the utter awareness that the clock is ticking relentlessly. Each day as I wake, just before opening my eyes, I say to myself, "Make this day worthwhile."

DIANA AT 25

When I look at this photo of myself, I see a young woman bold to the point of outrageous. I would look across an expanse of ocean and sneer at the prospect of sharks, heavy tides, and days of nonstop swimming. I would walk into CEOs' offices unannounced, cockily put my hands on my hips, and tell them that what I was going to accomplish would be historic, and they'd be lucky to be associated with it. I'd leave twenty minutes later with a check for $300,000 to fund the project.

CYBILL SHEPHERD

CYBILL AT 16

This picture was taken around the time I won the Miss Teenage Memphis Pageant. My cousin entered me in the pageant, filling out the whole form and making me sign it. I thought it was so stupid. I never wanted to be a beauty queen, even though I was raised to believe that you must aspire to be a homemaker or Miss America. I never wanted to be Jane; I always wanted to be Tarzan. I didn't want to vacuum the tree house and take care of Cheetah and Boy. I wanted to swing from the vines!

HER FAMOUSLY BEAUTIFUL FACE LAUNCHED HER CAREER, first as a beauty queen and cover girl, then as a movie star. In 1968, Memphis-born Cybill Shepherd captured the attention of the American public by winning *Model of the Year* from Stewart Models. Director Peter Bogdanovich spotted her on the cover of *Glamour* and cast her in a starring role in the 1971 film *The Last Picture Show.* Cybill soon became just as famous for her outrageously honest behavior off-screen, detailing her lovers (including Bogdanovich and Elvis) and appearing on *Late Night with David Letterman* clad only in a towel.

In her thirties, Cybill reinvented herself as a comedienne with her role as Maddie, the private eye in the TV series *Moonlighting.* After that, she starred as Cybill Sheridan, a middle-aged actress coping with life in youth-obsessed Hollywood in the CBS sitcom *Cybill,* for which she also served as executive producer. Cybill chronicled it all in her 2000 memoir, cleverly titled *Cybill Disobedience: How I Survived Beauty Pageants, Elvis, Sex, Bruce Willis, Lies, Marriage, Motherhood, Hollywood, and the Irrepressible Urge to Say What I Think.*

Passionate when it comes to politics, Cybill is a longtime supporter of the pro-choice political action committee Voters for Choice and an advocate for gay rights and women's issues. The devoted mother of three proclaims in her sassy southern voice: "The one thing no one can do better than me is 'Cybill.' By that I mean me being myself. I want to share that with the world. Life is short. I want to share that craziness, that honesty, that Cybill disobedience. I'm gonna keep swinging through the trees. Nothing is going to stop me!"

What has changed about your self-perception since you were a young woman?

Beauty is as beauty does. I feel my job is to develop self-compassion and practice loving kindness. I now meditate on the idea of no self. Letting go with love. That took a long time! I don't need a man anymore waiting in the wings!

MARTHA COOLIDGE

MARTHA IN HER EARLY 20s

As a young woman, I
struggled with insecurity and
self-criticism. I saw myself as
not smart enough, not pretty
enough, not athletic enough,
not talented enough—not a
winner. I'm much more
confident now and have a
greater appreciation of myself
and other people. I've gotten
out of my own way. Now I
can walk into a room or into
the spotlight and do my job.

BEFORE SOFIA COPPOLA BECAME A HOUSEHOLD NAME as a movie director, a fearless woman named Martha Coolidge helped pave the way for female directors in Hollywood. A protégée of Francis Ford Coppola, film director Martha Coolidge has quite a list of firsts on her impressive résumé. In 2001, for example, she became the first woman to head the powerful Directors Guild of America—a male-dominated bastion of the entertainment industry—in its sixty-year history. She also gave Oscar-winning actor Nicholas Cage his first starring role (in *Valley Girl*, 1983), and she directed actress Halle Berry in her first critically acclaimed role (the Emmy Award–winning television movie *Introducing Dorothy Dandridge*, 1999). And in 2000, Martha received Directors Guild of America and Emmy nominations for HBO's television movie *If These Walls Could Talk 2*.

Martha has never lost her love for the work itself. "For me, directing makes it all worthwhile—it is the thing I love doing." Her advice to young women who want to follow in her path: "Don't let others make rules, create your own rules. And when an opportunity comes, be ready. There is always an opportunity." At fifty-seven, she is still at the top of her game, having recently directed the romantic comedy *The Prince and Me,* starring Julia Stiles. Her proactive approach has helped her prevail as one of the most powerful women in Hollywood.

Who or what had the biggest influence on you?

The realization of my dream to become a director against all odds has given me tremendous confidence in everything that I do. The idea that I could accomplish my goals was seeded by my English/science teacher in seventh grade, Mr. Twitchell, who told me I should be able to do anything in life I wanted to do. It was shocking at the time but encouraging, too! I have never forgotten his words.

If you could go back and speak to your younger self, what piece of wisdom would you share?

Enjoy the process of doing more than aiming for a future result. How you live your life is as important as what you accomplish.

ANA PANIAGUA

ANA AT 24

This picture was taken just before I left to go to Los Angeles. Back then my children were the only things that made me happy. It was so hard to leave them.

ANA PANIAGUA IS A FEARLESS, HARDWORKING, FASCINATING ARTIST. Her life has not been easy. By her early twenties, she was already a single mother with three small children living in the poorest of conditions in El Salvador. Often she had barely enough to feed herself and her children. Like her mother before her, she was forced to lock her young children alone in the house each day while she did others' laundry, earning just enough money to buy that evening's dinner. Unwilling to let her children starve, she left her two oldest children with her sister, took her baby with her to California, and looked for work. As a live-in maid, she made a mere $600 a month, but she sent everything she could to El Salvador to support the children she had left behind. For years she worked hard at several jobs, determined to be reunited with her son and daughter. Eventually, she succeeded. Today her babies are grown adults with babies of their own, whom she helps raise. Still, Ana is as hardworking as ever.

Four years ago Ana discovered that she had an artistic talent. She started experimenting in oils and, to her surprise, began selling her unique paintings to collectors. Since then, she has had three gallery shows and is recognized for her primitive, colorful style. One day, when Ana was buying supplies in a posh art store, the clerk mistakenly assumed the oils and turpentine were for her boss. "Oh no," she proudly replied, "this is for me. *I* am the artist."

What do you hate about being in midlife but can laugh about anyway?

My tummy!

LAURA ROBINSON

LAURA AT 22

In this picture I was crowned the Fairest of the Fair. In my twenties it was all about auditioning, testing, seeking approval from others. In my thirties I was learning to live for others in a much different way—as a wife and mother. And now, in my forties, I'm learning to get my validation from within. And I don't need a crown to prove anything to anybody.

ACTRESS, INVENTOR, SINGER, SONGWRITER

RIGHT OUT OF COLLEGE, Laura became a well-known Canadian television actress. Young and naive, she soaked up all that entails fame and fun. It was an intoxicating time of prestige and recognition. But like most of us at twenty, Laura's success was measured by the approval of others—parents, producers, casting directors, colleagues, audiences. Next came the inventor phase. The enterprising twenty-six-year-old created the popular family board game Balderdash. This time her sense of accomplishment was measured by the financial success that came with the popularity of her game.

Now, at forty-seven, Laura is producing the television version of the game and, for her heart's sake, is following in the footsteps of her hero, Joni Mitchell, as she writes and records her own original acoustic music. She no longer looks outside herself to get validation, but believes in herself. She sings and writes songs for her own pleasure, with warm reception from nightclub audiences in Canada. When she enthusiastically told her lawyer about this new endeavor, he asked her if she wasn't just a little too old to be starting out as a singer. She valiantly replied, "I'm here to change that paradigm!"

If you could go back and speak to your younger self, what piece of wisdom would you share?

Keep moving, stay active, and always dance!

When did you realize that you were courageous?

When I had my first child. I was terrified during the hard part of labor and transition, and suddenly, I could not get the drugs because it was going too fast. I had to do it alone. The only way out of the pain was through it—like the old psychobabble adage—and it is true. When it was over, not only did I have my beautiful son to hold, I had this sense of pride and power in myself that has never left me. I did it! Amazing!

DR. RICKI POLLYCOVE

RICKI AT 25

Here I am at twenty-five,
entering my last year of
medical school, valuing inner
wisdom over simple beauty.
This was to be a theme
throughout my life.

RICKI POLLYCOVE BELIEVES THAT an early childhood in a rural town fortuitously exposed her to the natural world and gave her an appreciation for each individual's delicate balance. She received an impeccable medical education at University of California, Berkeley, and at the University of California, San Francisco, in an environment dominated by male students (only 6 percent of her graduating class was female). In spite of incredible pressure to "think like everyone else," she says she has always been "blessed or cursed with thinking outside the box." When she was put on probation in medical school for sitting on a patient's bed (twice), she knew that it would not be the last time she would pay a price for sticking to her guns. In her work as founder and director of California Pacific Medical Center Breast Health Center, and in her private practice as an obstetrician and gynecologist, she preaches a message of optimal care for women, which is sometimes controversial in a medical environment that is increasingly focused on the bottom line.

Ricki is a pioneer in the comprehensive approach to women's needs in midlife and beyond, incorporating psychology, nutrition, Chinese medicine, and alternative therapies into her patients' care. She is a longtime advocate of tailoring hormone therapy to each woman's unique situation. And in *Mother Nurture*, a book she coauthored, Pollycove offers a comprehensive program that helps women take care of themselves—and their families—physically and emotionally. As passionate as she is about her work and career, she feels her greatest accomplishment is being a good parent to her twenty-year-old daughter, Leah.

When did you realize you were courageous?

I have finally come to see that I am as well informed about important details of the depth and breadth of women's health as anyone out there. This has emboldened me to take a much more public stand, present my views so that they may be wrestled with by larger groups of colleagues, and hopefully make a greater difference in advancing the understanding and optimal health care of women, especially in midlife and beyond. This is my version of finding my voice.

LINDA GRAY

ACTRESS, GOODWILL AMBASSADOR

WHILE SHE IS MOST RECOGNIZED FOR HER WORK as the long-suffering Sue Ellen Ewing, the wife of J. R. on the popular prime-time soap opera *Dallas*, Linda Gray feels that her life really started after she played that role. "At forty, your life hasn't even begun," she says. "When do women buy into the notion that you have to go downhill? At forty, you are just getting finely tuned." Now, in her role as goodwill ambassador for the United Nations and advocate for global women's rights, she meets face to face with underprivileged and impoverished women around the world. "I have learned so much from these extraordinary, magnificent women," she says, "about the real value of life."

At age twenty-five, Linda remembers being told that she would soon be too old to continue modeling. Yet recently, she played Mrs. Robinson in a Broadway rendition of *The Graduate* "and took my clothes off—after the age of sixty, I might add!" When women concentrate on the past or the future, she says, they do a real disservice to themselves. "*This* is your moment," she says. "This is your delicious moment."

When did you realize you were courageous?

> I've always been courageous . . . only I'm not holding back anymore. I used to be shy.

What do you hate about being in midlife but can laugh about anyway?

> The extra layer of baby fat around my tummy that I blame on my kids . . . except they are in their thirties!!!

LINDA AT 18

I was just out of school and doing a few modeling gigs. My parents were not too happy that I had chosen this field to pursue, because "you know what kinds of girls go into these fields—like acting!" So then I knew I wanted to be an actor, but to keep peace I decided to stick with the modeling which was acceptable, sort of, back then.

ANN BELLES

ANN AT 18

During my high-school years, I spent almost all of my free time hanging out with the young patients at Fairview State Hospital for the Developmentally Disabled. There I witnessed abandoned children full of despair and hopelessness. It was then that I adjusted my dream a little. I changed from wanting to adopt orphan boys to, more specifically, wanting to adopt orphan boys with significant disabilities. One year later, I was parenting my first foster child.

ANN BELLES HAS KNOWN HER MISSION since she was a young girl. She saw the movie *Oliver!* when she was five years old, and the story of those abandoned, abused, and orphaned boys went straight to her heart. As soon as she turned nineteen, Ann began acting on a promise she made to herself to rescue and nurture children from all kinds of unfortunate circumstances. Today, she is still adopting boys from all over the world who have been labeled "unadoptable" because of their ages, ethnicities, and/or their cognitive, medical, and emotional disabilities. She and her husband, a quadriplegic himself, have adopted children from orphanages, nursing homes, hospitals, and abusive homes. Several of the children have been adopted from their own biological parents, who felt unequipped to raise a child with disabilities. Often these children are considered by various adoption experts to be "too damaged" to integrate into a family, but Ann proves the experts wrong.

Currently, she and Jim are parenting thirty adopted boys and young men who range in age from three to twenty-six years old. Ann's goal is to continue to rescue boys as well as find other adoptive parents for children who are waiting for their "forever family." Ann's tenacity to follow her dream demonstrates fearless love, courage, and patience.

Who or what had the biggest influence on how you view yourself?

Watching my kids grow and develop beyond the expectations of the "experts" made me aware that I can positively impact the lives of my boys in spite of the predictions of others.

What do you hate about being in midlife but can laugh about anyway?

It's still easy to get down on the floor and play with my kids; it's the getting back up that challenges me now that I am in my forties.

VICKI RANDLE

VICKI AT 21

I was getting 'hella play' for being 'fine' (I mean, c'mon, check out that Afro) and a great singer and musician. But I was so helpless then. Onstage I was paralyzed by fear, and unless I was actually singing, I barely even looked up or spoke. I had to drink a whole lot to get the courage even to do that. It would be years before I figured out that playing music to make other people like me wasn't a good enough reason. I came into my own when I began to realize that I loved it, and that was the only reason to be up there on the stage.

FEMALE PERCUSSIONISTS ARE A RARITY, especially female percussionists in high-profile positions, but Vicki Randle is a dynamic example of one. She performs fearlessly in the male-dominated world of musicians as the first and only woman in NBC's *The Tonight Show* band, a position she has held since 1992. She has spent much of her musical career—as a guitar player and vocalist as well as a percussionist—teaching her male counterparts how to respect her as both a fellow musician and a woman. Her efforts have paid off: She's won the admiration not only of others in the music industry, but of millions of Americans who watch her nightly as she rocks with the *Tonight Show* band and sings with the show's music director, Kevin Eubanks, during commercial breaks.

Vicki has been making music for more than three decades. From a girlhood debut in her Catholic church choir, she went on to tour and record with artists ranging from Aretha Franklin to Lionel Richie, all the while developing her own unique style influenced by music as diverse as folk, jazz, and opera. Now taking her turn in the spotlight, Vicki is proud to be a role model for so many of the young female viewers who shower her with fan mail. And in midlife, she has gotten over her fears of being in the vanguard: "I've always been courageous—sometimes in the form of foolhardiness—but until I matured, I was consumed with fear that forging ahead where few women had gone before would create ripples of backlash," she says. But Vicki has learned to challenge that fear by acting with integrity, honesty, kindness, and generosity, qualities that have also colored her definition of success. "If I'm not actively doing something to bring light and love and kindness to the world," she says, "the rest of my accomplishments aren't going to amount to much."

If you could go back and speak to your younger self, what piece of wisdom would you share?

No one is waking up in the morning thinking, "I wonder what Vicki needs today. How can I help her get it?" If you want something, you're going to have to stop waiting for others to make decisions for you and do the heavy labor yourself.

LARAINE NEWMAN

LARAINE AT 23

(with Gilda Radner)
We were having the time of
our lives that day. We were
having probably TOO much
fun. We were famous,
reasonably cute, and single.
It was Mardi Gras in New
Orleans, and we were
completely swept up in it.

LARAINE NEWMAN IS PROBABLY MOST REMEMBERED for being part of the original cast of *Saturday Night Live*. What she's most proud of is her relationship with her two daughters and her fifteen-year marriage to her husband, Chad. "I'm delighted that my life isn't all about me now," she says. "The pragmatic concerns of parenting and family have taken my ego completely out of the acting landscape. What a relief." When asked how she has become fearless about aging, she replied with her humor intact. "The biggest fear I ever had about aging was becoming socially and sexually invisible," she says. "When have you ever heard a hot young guy say something like "My, what a handsome woman!" "She's so vibrant for a grandmother, how sexy is that?" or "Let's go to that Eagles reunion concert and scam some mature chicks!"

At fifty-two Laraine has no hang-ups about being in midlife. She's not running to the cosmetic surgeon in order to feel good. She believes that now, more than ever, women have options: We have earning power, enough experience to know what we like and what we don't, and the courage to say so. "They say youth is wasted on the young," she reminds us. "I may be fifty-two on the outside, but in my head I'm twenty-five. I love where I'm at in my mind and spirit. I love understanding that, compared to the problems of most people in the world, there are very few big deals in my life. I feel more comfortable in my own skin, sagging though it may be. Does that mean I rejoice in the distribution of body fat that comes with age? The need for naps? Rushing into a room with wild intent only to forget what it was? Hell, no—but I don't fear it."

When did you realize you were courageous?

When I learned to walk through fear and despair and accept change.

MY FEARLESS FRIEND

PHOTO

FOUNDATIONS

Here is a listing of charities and other organizations founded by fearless women featured in this book.

Gloria Allred | WERLDEF
(Women's Equal Rights Legal Defense and Education Fund)
A referral line to help educate women about their legal rights and assist them in vindicating those rights by providing access to the courts.

(323) 653-8087

Ann Belles | FRIENDS OF FIRST STEP
Distributes donated funds and supplies to assist children and adults with disabilities to live successfully in their communities. Funds are used for medical equipment and treatment, continuing education, housing, and support staff.

The Silcock Family
9121 Atlanta Ave., Box # 633
Huntington Beach, CA 92646
Fax: (714) 963-0187 | www.allourboys.com

Angie Bunch | CULTURE SHOCK DANCE
Worldwide professional hip-hop dance troupes and nonprofit youth outreach organization that cultivates self-worth, dignity, and respect for all.

www.cultureshockdance.org

Kathy Eldon | CREATIVE VISIONS
A film and television production company dedicated to supporting "media that matters."

8539 Sunset Boulevard, Suite #4-122
West Hollywood, CA 90069
Fax: (310) 289-5037 | www.creativevisions.org

Leeza Gibbons | LEEZA'S PLACE
Creates intimate, safe settings to offer support for those newly diagnosed with memory disorder and their caregivers.

The Leeza Gibbons Memory Foundation
3050 Biscayne Boulevard, Suite 908
Miami, FL 33137
(888) OK-LEEZA | www.leezasplace.com

Lois Lee | CHILDREN OF THE NIGHT
Assists children between the ages of eleven and seventeen who are forced to prostitute on the streets for food and a place to sleep.

14530 Sylvan Street
Van Nuys, CA 91411
(818) 908-4474 | Help Hotline: (800) 551-1300
www.childrenofthenight.org

CCH Pounder
ARTISTS FOR A NEW SOUTH AFRICA
Dedicated to combating the AIDS pandemic and advancing equality in South Africa.

www.ansafrica.org

BORIBANA MUSEUM
The first contemporary art museum in Dakar, Senegal.

Musée Boribana
BP 8902, Dakar, Senegal
Phone: 011 221 8204115
www.boribanamuseum.org

Stefanie Powers | WILLIAM HOLDEN
WILDLIFE FOUNDATION
Funds education programs that reach out to Kenya's population, particularly its children, and serve as a backup to specific animal conservation and habitat preservation.

whwildlife@aol.com | http://www.whwf.org

Gilda Radner | GILDA'S CLUB
Through clubhouses around the nation, a community of support is created to help people of all ages with cancer learn from one another to live their lives fully.

Gilda's Club Worldwide
322 Eighth Avenue, Suite 1402
New York, NY 10011
Fax: (917) 305-0549
info@gildasclub.org | www.gildasclub.org

Victoria Rowell | THE ROWELL FOSTER
CHILDREN'S POSITIVE PLAN
Awards long-term fine arts and academic scholarships to foster youth.

The Rowell Foster Children's Positive Plan
16633 Venture Boulevard, Suite 1450
Encino, CA 91436
(323) 857-1717 | www.rowellfosterchildren.org

Marilyn Tam
US FOUNDATION
Facilitates global action to address social, economic, and environmental issues.

Us Foundation
P.O. Box 5780
Santa Barbara, CA 93150
www.usfoundation.org

UNIVERSAL FORUM OF CULTURES
BARCELONA 2004
Gathers people from all societies to participate in creating a better planet based on principles of cultural diversity and economic and environmental sustainability.

www.barcelona2004us.org

Lynne Twist | SOUL OF MONEY INSTITUTE
Assists individuals and organizations in their relationship with money.

Soul of Money Institute
3 Fifth Ave.
San Francisco, CA 94118
(585) 242-0208 | www.soulofmoney.org

Catherine Curry-Williams | SHANE'S
INSPIRATION
Creates universally accessible playgrounds for children of all abilities.

Shane's Inspiration
4804 Laurel Canyon #542
Valley Village, CA 91604
(818) 752-5676 | www.shanesinspiration.org

ACKNOWLEDGMENTS

We would like to acknowledge and thank the following people on our team: Joe Croyle, studio manager, and also an amazing gourmet chef. Thanks for keeping us all fed throughout this entire book project and for your love, patience, and support. Isabella Way, associate producer; Franco Sama, production coordinator; and Harlan Boll, talent coordinator. To our great photography assistants: Martha Altamirano, Wendy Hudson, Viki Van Den Barselaar, and Lonnie Morris. And the rest of our team: Dennis Holahan, legal assistance; Susan Heyman, accountant; and to Isgo Lepejian—thank you for your beautiful prints of these photographs and all your support through the years. For technical support: Manny's Camera Repair, Gregg Leon.

Thanks to all the people who donated their time and services: **HAIR AND MAKEUP:** Deva D'ull (*Andrea Thompson (cover), Erin Brockovich, Beth Broderick, Brooke Medicine Eagle, Lonnie Ali, Judy Weider*); Donna Gast (*CCH Pounder, Laraine Newman, Linda Gray, Vicki Randle*); Elizabeth Donaldson (*Lois Lee, Gloria Allred, Angie Bunch*); Sandy Williams (*Martha Coolidge, Ivana Chubbuck, Laura Robinson, Vicki Vyeniello, Ana Paniagua*); Lisa Marie Ponzio (hairstylist for Warren Tricomi Salon) and Nicole Bryl (*Joan Lunden*); Robin Siegel and Jonathon Hanousek (*Kathy Najimy*); Nancy Morrison and Sparkle (*Victoria Rowell*); Cathy Highland (*Melissa Manchester*); Eric Barnard (*Cybill Shepherd*); Taylor Babaian (*Joni Mitchell*). **FURNISHINGS**: Marlow, Mark J Low, Jennifer, Cheryl M Low. Dove provided by Monique Monros, magician.

We would like to thank the following people for their help in transforming this book from a dream to a reality: Sam and Mary Haskell, Donna Guillumme-Brown, Chris Newman, Babette Perry, Heidi Schaeffer, Michael Alden, Dawn Thomas, Read Jackson, Diane Perlmutter, Gilda's Club, Brad Seeley, Rick Hobbs, Charles "Val" Valentino, Cathy McAuley, John Howard Swain and Marsha Mercant, Full Circle Productions in San Fransisco, John Esterle, Melinda Kristofich, Vincent Arcuri, Stacy Gordon, Nick Byassee, Daniel Passer, Toni Ann Rossi, Minda Burr, Claudia Kagen, Cheryl Bianchi, Richard and Mary Kentz. And of course, to all of our friends and family for their continuing love, support, understanding, and laughs.

Special thanks to Melanie Falick, along with the rest of the STC team, and Susi Oberhelman for great design. Thank you all for allowing this project to reach the world.

And finally, Special, Special, Special Thanks and Love to Arielle Ford and Brian Hilliard, for seeing us through this amazing but incredibly difficult labor of love.

Dedicated to the memory of
GILDA RADNER,
and to the many fearless
women who have lost their
lives prematurely to cancer.

Laraine Newman and Gilda Radner, 1976

Gilda's Club was established in
honor of comedian Gilda Radner,
who died of ovarian cancer in 1989,
and whose spirit lives on in
Gilda's Clubs everywhere. A portion
of the royalties from *Fearless Women:
Midlife Portraits* will go to benefit
Gilda's Club Worldwide, whose
mission is to provide meeting places
where men, women, and children
living with cancer and their families
and friends can join with others to
build emotional and social support as
a supplement to medical care.

1-888-GILDA-4-U

Gilda's Club Worldwide
322 Eighth Avenue, Suite 1402
New York, NY 10011

info@gildasclub.org
www.gildasclub.org

Published in 2005 by
Stewart, Tabori & Chang
115 West 18th Street
New York, NY 10011
www.abramsbooks.com

Canadian Distribution:
Canadian Manda Group
One Atlantic Avenue, Suite 105
Toronto, Ontario M6K 3E7
Canada

Library of Congress Cataloging-in-Publication Data
is on file with the Library of Congress

ISBN: 1-58479-412-7

The text of this book was composed in
Trajan, Fairfield, and Folio.

Designed by Susi Oberhelman

Printed in Singapore

10 9 8 7 6 5 4 3 2 1

FIRST PRINTING

Stewart, Tabori & Chang is a subsidiary of
LA MARTINIÈRE